SHUT DOWN the HOME OFFICE

Other Books by the Author:

IDEA TRACKING
THE MODERN SALES MANAGER'S SECRET WEAPON
MEMOS TO MANAGEMENT

SHUT DOWN the HOME OFFICE

Hands-on Market-driven Management for the Nineties

Frank A. Armstrong

 DONALD I. FINE, INC.   NEW YORK

Library of Congress Cataloging-in-Publication Data

Armstrong, Frank A. (Frank Alexander), 1921–
    Shut down the home office : hands-on, market-driven management for the nineties / Frank Armstrong.
        p.   cm.
    ISBN: 1-55611-248-3
    1. Industrial management—United States—Case studies.   2. Success in business—United States—Case studies.   I. Title.
HD70.U5A78   1991
658.4—dc20   90-56061
                      CIP

Manufactured in the United States of America

10 9 8 7 6 5 4 3 2

Designed by Irving Perkins Associates

To Dorothy, Mark, Lina Jean,
Christine, Michael, Jane,
Jay, Ret, Wesley, Geoff and David

CONTENTS

There Is No Shortage of Talent in American Business. It Is the Organizational Methods That Are No Longer Effective

AMERICAN MANAGEMENT and organizational methods and styles of the past 50 years are not working now. They cannot be fixed just by cutting back excessive organizational costs. There has been plenty of that in the 1980s. The methods of organization have to change. The way American management thinks has to change. Here are some of the key elements of contemporary American management methods that have to be attacked and changed:

- The use by management of staff to "keep in touch" with what is going on in the market.
- The excessive use of committees to evaluate problems and provide solutions.

- The burgeoning number of meetings that are generated by the burgeoning amount of staff.
- The massive output of reports on every conceivable aspect of the business, including many that are not important.
- The use of top management time simply to manage the work of the home-office organization.
- The layer upon layer of management (up to ten layers in some businesses) that slows or stops the flow of decisions and actions.

Most of this organizational form is a uniquely American development that evolved as corporations grew and combined. The intent was to provide managers with the important information they needed to lead and direct a business. It worked when the economy was expanding rapidly, when production and supply were increasing, when demand was strong and when competition came mainly from other American companies.

But this American business environment has clearly changed. The problem probably became urgent with the OPEC oil price rise in 1973 and the bad times that continued for American business for the ten years that ended with the recession of 1981–1982. Overstaffing, unproductive workers and outdated plants left many American companies vulnerable before a flood of high-quality products pouring in from West Germany, East Asia and Japan.

Believe it! Here are a few statistics to confirm that American business leadership had become soft. In 1975 America led machine tool production around the world. By 1985 America had virtually stopped exporting machine tools. Japanese and German machine tools became standard in U.S. production. American share of semiconductor fabrication went from 60 percent to just over 30 percent. Memory chips went from 86 percent to 15 percent.

American companies dropped out of consumer electronic products. We no longer produce home radios, black-and-white TVs, phonographs, cassette players and we make only a small part of the color TV. American companies do not make VCRs or CD players. This trouble had been developing for years. Companies had become slow-reacting while they were dominant. Management was self-satisfied, terribly overstaffed and overorganized.

Suddenly American business was engulfed by competitors from overseas. In industry after industry foreign competitors became the major players. They are tough, aggressive and smart.

All this has produced a major change in this American business environment, but it has not produced significant changes in the way many businesses operate. For example, you hear volumes of talk these days about hands-on management, suggesting that executives are out there and down there somewhere getting in touch with reality. But most of it is just talk.

Management feet are still imbedded in the cement of the home office. And why not? That's where you find the fancy offices, the closed doors, the big conference rooms and the legions of staff people whose job is to gather information and prepare long reports.

You can see it in many large companies. But this trend has been picked up and adopted by medium and small companies as well. It goes beyond the trappings of power and authority. The damaging characteristic rests in the home office orientation, which says clearly, "This is what it is all about. Here's where the knowledge is. Here is where all the decisions and actions are created."

I've seen this attitude pervade business during twenty-five years of working in and for a wide variety of companies. Following are some specific examples. This is not a long list, but there are enough cases to exemplify the nature of this problem. In retrospect, some of the problems appear so obvious that it is hard to believe that they could not have been seen and easily avoided.

A best-selling business book in 1982, *In Search of Excellence*, by Tom Peters and Robert H. Waterman Jr., who had been associated with the consulting firm of McKinsey & Co., did much to support the idea that the old organizational methods of the 1950–1980 period are still effective. But most of the book's research was done in the 1970s. The examples of "excellence" in the book support the "old way." The book cites as examples companies that have since had severe problems, such as Wang, Lockheed, Caterpillar, Deere, Tupperware and Atari. There are plenty of other examples (not included in that book) such as General Motors, Del Monte and Eastern Airlines, that make an eloquent argument *against* the proposition presented by that book. Times have changed. The marketplace has changed. And Tom Peters has changed. He has since written a book that confirms the state of "chaos" in American business. Now here are some examples from my own experience:

- I can still hear the General Motors top managers at the bar of the Detroit Athletic Club roaring with laughter at the idea that the "beetles" and "bugs" would have any impact on the U.S. automotive market. That was in 1972, just before the Arab oil embargo, which changed everything we knew about cars and long after the VW had become a significant entry into the American car market.
- I saw almost no awareness by top management at Del Monte of the profound changes taking place in the food industry in the 1960s and 1970s. Del Monte then had 70 percent of the shelf space in supermarkets for canned fruits and vegetables. Most of the top people were oriented to production, to crops, to canneries. They were more like farmers than marketing men and spent little time in the marketplace. It is sad to see the result of this thinking in the state of Del Monte today.
- The generals and admirals who "retired" into business at top management levels found the layered structure of American business familiar and comforting. They liked the "pyramid," the centralization, the staff, the headquarters dominance. They rarely were seen in the marketplace, and few of them did outstanding work in business. I personally observed General Lauris Norstadt, ex-head

of NATO, as president of Owens Corning Fiber-
glas. He was a fine military leader with impeccable
personal qualities. But he knew nothing about the
business of the company and contributed little or
nothing to its operating decisions.

- I watched Westinghouse stay in the small-
appliance business for fifteen long years after it
became clear that this business was not right for
the company. Why? Its managers kept doing what
they had been doing and top executives never
bothered to take a close look at this particular business segment and at the changing marketplace.
- When I heard a Buick top management man say in
1970, "My only competition is with Oldsmobile
and Pontiac. Hell, those Mercurys and Dodges
aren't in the game," I realized how myopic and
disengaged from the marketplace and from competition the GM division's top management had
become.
- I saw complete sales, marketing and advertising
plans delivered to the outer office of the chairman
of Schenley Distilleries. No personal presentation
was permitted. The material was reviewed in private and in total isolation from the marketplace.
- In the world of advertising, Marion Harper,
founder of Interpublic Group, pushed, pulled,
drove the mega-agency to a dominant position in
the industry. He surrounded himself with a huge,
highly paid staff. Harper worked mainly with his
staff, rarely with front-line people and almost
never with the clients. This isolation from the mar-

ketplace eventually proved disastrous for the agency and for Harper. The excessive costs from preening luxuries and staffing hurt. But it was mistake after mistake by Harper and his staff that produced a tragic ending. Huge losses forced the banks to step in. Harper was forced out and never recovered from the shock.

- Everyone knows about the marketing mistake of the century by Coca Cola with the *instantaneous national introduction of New Coke*. There's little doubt that this change was made and supported by careful evaluation, extensive research and extensive counseling with important bottlers. All the bases were covered except the marketplace, the drinkers of "regular" Coke. They only had one thing to say after the fact: a painful "No." There was too much inside and not enough outside thinking.

Years ago I decided to "pass" on the big-business type of organization. Since then, I have spent twenty years as an entrepreneur. I've built from the ground up three separate and successful businesses in vitamins, specialty food ingredients and soft drinks.

Over these years I've bought businesses and combined many of them for greater efficiency. I've had a mixture of hits and misses. I've raised many millions in capital on my signature and credentials (with no junk bonds). I've become addicted to cash flow after taxes. And I am committed to the idea of running any business on a *market-driven basis*, from the place where the business takes place.

I know that the term "market-driven" has become a battered cliché lately. But that is because many of the managers and consultants who use it don't really understand what it means, how it works and why it is the only way to run a business these days if you want to be around at the turn of the century.

General Motors just appointed a new CEO. Let us hope he really is a new one and not just another punch-press version of the last several. The one thing that turns out to be a common aspect of all these people is, probably literally as well as figuratively, that the bottoms of their shoes are barely worn. They just don't go anywhere that doesn't have thick carpets or velvety greens. They already know the GM way of doing things. They haven't had to learn anything. Which is, of course, why GM may not be around at the turn of the next century, certainly not in its present form.

It is interesting to note that more than one of the accounts of the accession of Robert Stempel to the top job at GM suggested that his first step should be to shut down the fourteenth floor of the General Motors Building in Detroit, the corporation's renowned and forbidding home office fortress.

When I talk about market-driven, I don't mean some vague notion of doing market research or meeting with your regional sales managers to get a handle on things. I mean running your company from the marketplace, from where the action is. It took me a while to understand the difference between talking about it and doing it. But I have done it, and it works.

In the process of doing it, the guidelines for a different style of management emerged. There is often more to learn from the failures than from the successes. Some of the failures came because of the people involved. But, more often, they come from a lack of deep knowledge of the particular marketplace and how the company operated in that place and in that time.

This book defines specific methods that work in today's hypercompetitive business world. The examples are typically about successful operations that are run by new-style leaders who are market-driven and who minimize the importance of a "home office" remote from the marketplace.

CHAPTER *2*

An Example of a Market-Driven Organization

THE COMPANY I am talking about is my own, The Monarch Company. It is a franchise company in the soft-drink industry, medium-sized, and ranks in the top three involved in marketing brands and flavors for non-cola soft drinks. These include fruit flavors, mixers and root beers. The brands of Monarch include *Dad's Root Beer*, *Bubble Up*, *NuGrape*, *Nesbitts*, *Frostie*, *Suncrest* and the oldest soft-drink brand in the country, *Moxie*. Monarch sells to and services more than eight hundred soft drink bottling plants across the country. There are Monarch brands sold in every state and in forty countries around the world. Monarch sells bottlers the flavor concentrates for all the Monarch brands.

The business has been formed over many years by combining individual brands into one operating company. For a time it bumped along with modest growth of 4 to 6 percent a year, which reflected the overall growth of this segment of the soft-drink industry. And for years it had a typical organization with a management group, support staff, national sales organization and technical staff.

Six years ago we changed all that. This was motivated by an awareness that significant changes were being made by some of the most aggressive and successful companies.

Here are the twenty-five organizational and operational features of The Monarch Company as it has been run since 1985.

1. Monarch has no home-office management.
2. The main functions of the Atlanta office are the administrative and financial operations of the company.
3. Management spends an average of more than 70 percent of its time in markets working directly with franchise bottlers.
4. The top six sales people all have specific key bottlers assigned for personal in-market contact every quarter.
5. These key bottlers account for 70 percent of Monarch's total sales.
6. The marketing programs come directly from constant contact with bottlers and retailers in the markets.
7. Marketing programs are localized to fit the specific needs of particular markets and the bottlers and the retailers.

8. A promotion group services the field sales organization and franchised bottlers.
9. Responses to *competitors* are handled on a market-by-market basis.
10. Bottler calls by key management people are made with Monarch's area sales manager of the company.
11. Area managers are among the best paid and best supported field people in the industry.
12. Monarch knows that the power to produce sales growth is in the markets and not in the home office.
13. When a problem develops, Monarch sends people to the field to seek solutions or brings in area managers to meet and solve the problems.
14. New products originate from specific opportunities that come directly from the marketplace.
15. Monarch's flavor development laboratories develop products for individual customers and individual market needs.
16. Product quality control of flavor concentrates is achieved in plants using the most sophisticated and automated technical and production equipment.
17. Market research in the traditional sense is rarely used. Instead, Monarch management provides the needed information and adds the instinctive judgment required in a particular situation.
18. Monarch computers provide comprehensive sales and financial information on every aspect

of the business. Sales by brand, by size, by customer, by area, by salesman.

19. The major form of communication with the market is person-to-person, face-to-face.
20. The telephone is the next most important form of communication.
21. Paper communication is used mainly for administrative control purposes.
22. All management people exchange all key customer contact reports on a continuing basis.
23. Monarch is a working, gunning example of a market-driven business in the real sense of that term.
24. Monarch's sales have grown 500 percent since this market-driven program was put in place in 1985.
25. Monarch cash flow has kept pace precisely with the sales growth and is more than five times the cash flow of 1985.

CHAPTER *3*

Companies That Are Beginning To "Shut Down" The Home Office

KENNETH IVERSON (CEO of *Nucor*, the minimill steel innovator), says, "The most important thing American industry needs to do is reduce the number of management layers. We have four management layers. We have a foreman, and the foreman goes directly to a department head, and the department head goes directly to the general manager, and he goes directly to this office."

William Woodside (CEO of *Primerica Corp.*), says, "We have the poorest productivity growth in any Western industrialized country. And managerial ineptitude has put us into this box. The way to get higher productivity is to train better managers and have fewer of them. Four years ago we had more than twelve hundred people at corporate headquarters. We're coming down to two-fifty."

When Charles Ames took over as head of $400 million *Acme Cleveland,* he cut corporate headquarters staff from 120 to 50.

Brunswick Corporation, the Chicago-based sporting goods maker, cut management layers in half and turned a losing situation around.

Ford Motor Co., in an effort to become more competitive with the Japanese, has cut more than 26 percent of its middle management staff.

Chaparral Steel has prospered with just four layers of management for years.

Mars Inc., the family-owned candy maker, runs the business with a thirty-person central management group.

Lincoln Electric, with electronic parts sales of a half billion, makes do with a management control ratio of 1 to 100 and yet achieves greater productivity than the industry average.

Schlumberger, the $6 billion diversified oil service company, runs its worldwide empire with a corporate staff of just under one hundred.

Emerson Electric has around fifty thousand employees but has fewer than a hundred executives at headquarters.

McKinsey & Co., the giant consulting firm, examined thirty-eight advanced manufacturing technology

1. *The cost of excessive home-office staffing is not the problem. It is what the staff can do to the business that hurts.*

systems. They concluded, according to *Boardroom Reports*: "The first step in accomplishing successful plant-floor implementation of new manufacturing approaches is the clearing out of all the middle managers and support service layers that clog the wheels of change."

CHAPTER **4**

Shut Down the Home Office

To call for shutting down the home office, and I mean that literally, is not to say that there should be no place to come home to, no place for the accounting department, the controller, the personnel people and the other necessary business support functions to perform.

But the home office, as it is conceived in too many companies, must change its form and size and function in the company. This is not a matter of playing with words. Changing the form of the home office is an essential part of the process of changing the character, the culture of the company. It will eliminate the fortress mentality that has infected American business and that is destroying many companies, small ones as well as giants.

This change in the form and function of the home office can take a variety of forms to match the particular needs of a business. But, if management is going to do the job differently, then the function of the home office will automatically be changed. It will cease to be the base of power and prestige. That base will shift to the customer and to the marketplace. The reduction of home-office staffs is a measure that has been adopted by some companies and has been forced on others by the economic demands of the times and the business.

Peter Drucker, in his classic, *The Practice of Management*, recommended seven layers as the maximum necessary for any organization. But, that was in 1954, a different era. Today the push is to three layers with five as the maximum.

Smaller companies, under $50 million in sales, have almost always avoided large staff organizations. They can't afford the luxury. For example, in a survey by McKinsey, such companies have no staff operations or departments at all to perform the following functions (shown as a percentage of those that don't have them):

No Government Relations	80 percent
No Internal Communications	64 percent
No Public Affairs	68 percent
No Investor Relations	55 percent
No Corporate Planning	40 percent
No Legal Affairs	33 percent

In *World Class Manufacturing*, Richard Schonberger returns time and again to the topic of "better support with [fewer] people," based on his extensive observations of hundreds of changes in structure at the factory level of organization. One chapter on staff roles, for instance, discusses "better maintenance with fewer

people in the plant maintenance department" (operators do their own maintenance, faster and cheaper,
when prevention of failure is considered), better quality with fewer people in the quality-control department. Self-inspection, with appropriate training,
becomes the norm. Dana Corp. has a plant in Nebraska
that employs 120 people. The organization is simple:
120 people, one plant manager, and that is all.

While he was still associated with GM, Ross Perot
observed, "In Pontiac, GM executive parking garages
are heated, while the poor guys who work in the plant
freeze their tails off walking to work in the snow. It
costs $140,000 a year to heat one parking garage. I'd
shut that thing down. It has nothing to do with managing and selling cars."

Fortune magazine reports on James Reid, running
an exceptionally profitable auto components maker,
Standard Products: "He drives a compact Oldsmobile.
His company, on the verge of the Fortune 500, is still
run from a drab two-story brick building in Cleveland's
warehouse district. But, he says, 'I can do as much
thinking here as in an office fifty times this size.' "

ADP has more than a dozen individual businesses
that are run with a high degree of independence and
with almost no home-office staff control. ADP maintains offices in more than a hundred cities. Each local
manager is responsible for customer development and
service as well as financial performance.

The New York *Times* recently reported that anti-
bureaucrat Ken Iverson of Nucor Corp. maintains an
"executive dining room: It's the Chinese restaurant or

2. When the home office "closes" and executives take to the road, big changes take place in who is talking to whom and in what terms.

the delicatessen (usually the deli) in the shopping center across the street from Nucor's headquarters in
Charlotte, North Carolina."

The Center for Accounting and Information Services is my suggestion for a more precise name for
what should become of the old home office. Accounting takes in all of the related financial services. The
computers still run. The payables and receivables still
function. It is in the office of management that the
significant change takes place. This change will produce others. With the base of power no longer station-
ary (but instead moving with the executives), other
changes follow. The size of the staff decreases as the
need to supply management with plans and information services decreases. The marketing people work in
the market, probably more than anyone else. Sales
management will leave town and only come back
when there is a need to consolidate selling and production plans. Production people will be at the plants
where their products are made. The idea of an executive vice-president of production working at the
home office so he can be close to the top man will be
obliterated.

The phenomenon of "management talking to management" declines. Communication on almost any
subject changes from general to specific. The consideration of what to do about a competitive product will
change from the notion that "something must be done
to make us more competitive," to the specific direction
needed to achieve this objective. Working in the marketplace and with customers will produce significant

directives about what needs to be done to make the entire operation more effective and more profitable.

Vital current information from the marketplace will guide the decisions that affect the people in the company at all levels. Do what the market demands or get out. Those who can do the job survive and prosper and grow. It is not a matter of who likes whom. It comes down to the basics of getting results in the marketplace.

In his landmark study of federal government efficiency, Peter Grace, the former CEO of W.R. Grace & Co., identified a phenomenon that can best be called the bureaucratic flood. It can overwhelm any kind of organization. Grace found many departments and jobs that, when eliminated, had no negative effect on the work of the government. These cuts ran to $110 billion, only 30 percent of Grace's total recommendations. Grace found entire departments with functions that were no longer needed and that had become obsolete because of the work of other departments in other branches of the government. Useless workers continued to work diligently to produce reports without a purpose.

We have come to expect this situation in government, a bureaucracy that we recognize has a life and power of its own. Mikhail Gorbachev, in his work to effect change in the Soviet Union, has said, "We all should seriously busy ourselves with bringing to completion this work to dismantle the mechanism of decline, of decay, of deceleration. All delegations show that bureaucratism still shows its teeth, so to speak, resists and puts spokes in the wheels. This is a wide-spread phenomenon."

The truth is that this same phenomenon, this seemingly unstoppable flood of bureaucracy, affects business organizations as well. Everyone picked on General Motors as its market share declined. But it took massive share losses and massive profit declines before the company looked within and began cutting back the huge bureaucracy that it had built from the end of World War II into the 1980s.

Consider a typical example in corporate life. The legal departments in many large companies started with the increase in regulation of business. Management unquestionably needed more advice on legal matters that affected the business. This need expanded to include taxes, securities, unions, employees, retirement, product liability, working conditions, and so on. So the legal department came into existence, probably starting with one lawyer. It made sense. But the one lawyer couldn't do all the legal work so the company continued to use outside legal counsel as well. Then the legal department expanded to include lawyers specializing in the various fields that impinged on the business. This legal work became so extensive that the decision-making process began to slow. The legal department became a self-controlled source of power that even the most aggressive top executives were hesitant to cross swords with. The ultimate power sometimes was the legal department's warning that a certain course could lead to a criminal action and "someone can end up in jail." (In the period from 1977 to 1989, the number of lawyers increased 14 percent while the general population grew by just 6 percent.)

Next might come an embryo marketing research department. First there was a marketing research director who, when he needed more information, consulted with outside research companies. Eventually the director acquired a headquarters staff of detached professionals engulfed in their own work on new products, advertising, packaging, customer profiles, economic trends, new market opportunities, consumer focus studies, sales results, competitive sales results and so on. Inevitably this process went beyond the practical need for information.

The professionals who staff these home-office departments develop their skills but often lose touch with the mainstream of the business itself. They rarely doubt their findings and tend to isolate themselves from the realities of the marketplace.

This tendency can be compounded by interaction with other departments. The early success of NASA's project organization structure brought a new idea, the matrix, another form of centralization. Every group was to be connected to every other group. Organization charts reveal blizzards of dotted lines. The purpose was to gain support that would come from coordinating everything and everyone with everything else and everyone else. That tends to produce official, bureaucratic positions on just about everything. That sense of interaction almost certainly contributed to the failure of the O-ring that resulted in the destruction of the Challenger shuttle. The part's problem was not corrected after repeated signs of its existence. The many groups within the organization were too busy "communicating" with each other to make a *decision* about a potential problem.

Robert Hall, in a recent article entitled "Attaining Manufacturing Excellence," writes, "Management excellence cannot come from fragmented contributions by various functional staffs; that is, if quality assurance has exclusive jurisdiction over a quality program, if production control has an inventory program, and so on. Each staff seeks to impose another set of techniques, each set demanding adjustments and attention from an already choked line organization. Only so much can be assimilated at a time, and it should be cohesive. Japanese are good integrators. Americans are accustomed to thinking that integration of a company is only in one place—at the top, where strategy is made."

CHAPTER 5

Cut the Staff, Save the Money and Much More

PART OF the problem with the development of huge staffs comes from the drive to reach optimum levels of performance. The "optimizer" is also a "centralizer." General Motors, despite an organizational structure that purported to be a classic example of decentralization, maintains an all-powerful centralized system of control. Virtually every decision, even down to such matters as redesigning a defective hood lock, had to go downtown to the General Motors Building in Detroit for years, despite so-called divisional autonomy.

We have also seen central control take command in other corporations that, for example, run their marketing activities with a corporation-wide advertising budget. And in finance, computers have permitted complex centralized control.

The same sort of thing happened in the 1970s when

29

mounting oil prices caused transportation costs to rise precipitously. This led directly to centralized staff work to measure all transportation costs to optimize efficiencies.

Each such development produces more central staff work. That in turn produces more requests for information from the line people, more demand for the coordination of one report with another. And so it goes, on and on with more central control of information, more staff people. The belief that there is a need for more order forces the development of committees and finally a committee to coordinate the committees.

Here's an example in a company that I have worked with that shows what can happen when a large home-office staff is functioning at full force:

- Some 75 percent of all working hours were spent in meetings.
- Most meetings were scheduled well ahead of time.
- The meetings were attended by an average of twenty people usually drawn from different staff levels.
- The meetings featured chart and slide material filled with facts and figures presented by junior staff people.
- The purpose of the meetings was to produce decisions (many of which were never acted upon).

As the home-office people and paper flood rises, management finds itself trapped. It must supervise all the work of all the disciplines of all the meetings and all the committees.

In contrast, Bennett Cerf, cofounder of Random House, the book publisher, would leave the room the moment he sensed that a meeting might start. Cerf felt that meetings were the worst possible way to make decisions that would determine which books to publish.

Too many managers in a home-office staff environment come to depend on instant information on every conceivable subject. This often will result in massive amounts of plainly irrelevant though accurate information.

In huge staff organizations, people pay inordinate attention to titles and formalities so they can deal with the politics. Tightly structured hierarchies come very close to a class system. At one major financial company, for instance, the hierarchy runs from Class 20, for those with a high-school diploma, all the way up to Class 45 for the highest vice-presidential level.

If you have been caught in such an organization, you know the problem of reviewing and digesting the torrent of facts and figures that come from many different sources. A computer can take that much input, but what about the mind of management? Eventually the drowning process takes place. Home-office staffs take control of the business on a daily basis, though nobody planned it this way.

Conventional thinking says that somehow the key management people will absorb this mass of informa-

3. *What is often missing is the
sense of priority among all the
opportunities and problems
of the business.*

tion, sorting out the key factors and providing direction for the future of the business. It would seem that so much information would result in more precision in the decision-making process, but just the opposite occurs. In fact, this situation ignores the enormous power and momentum that the staff accumulates over time. Very talented and forceful people are at work in staff departments. They must be listened to. An organization can be fettered by the thinking of its staff. Top management people are not always free to avoid staff output and develop their own information and do their own thinking.

There is far too much information, and it is splintered and divided and divided again. With so many factors to consider, it becomes almost impossible to sort out the ones that make a difference. What occurs is a slow but steady growth of generalized decisions and generalized actions.

Some years ago, a major tool manufacturer began to consider conversion to the metric system for tool design. An initial research report covered all of the nations of the world using the metric system as well as the few that had continued to use the British system. There were also numerous federal government reports on the efficiency of the metric system. The facts piled up. Several departments in the home office had a voice in the matter. Outside consultants were retained to research, evaluate and recommend.

In the face of this enormous flood of information, management made the decision to prepare for the changeover to the metric system for a new line of tools.

This required an investment in new designs, tooling and production equipment as well as the need to retain the previous product line. The required new capital was raised with a bond issue. All of this occurred in 1980, but the change to the metric system for U.S. tools is still many years in the future. This is a classic example of too many facts obscuring the practical aspect of a major decision, because nobody made a serious effort to find out what was going on in the rest of the industry and among customers. Had they done so, they no doubt would have discovered that their "well-thought-out" decision was a mistake.

In the 1930s, the legendary General Motors chairman Alfred P. Sloan turned self-critical, observing that "in practically all our activities we seem to suffer from the inertia resulting from our great size.... There are so many people involved and it requires such a tremendous effort to put something new into effect that a new idea is likely to be considered insignificant in comparison with the effort that it takes to put it across.... Sometimes I am almost forced to the conclusion that General Motors is so large and its inertia so great that it is impossible for us to be leaders."

Structural economist Frederick Scherer studied the fate of fifteen subsidiaries of conglomerates that had been sold to former managers. He reported in his own research paper that fourteen of them showed substantial improvements in net profit—despite the burden of debt incurred in the buyouts. Among the reasons for the improvement, Scherer notes these: "Cost-cutting opportunities that had previously gone unexploited were seized. . . . Inexpensive computer services were found to substitute for expensive in-house operations. Make-versus-buy decisions were reevaluated, and lower cost alternatives were embraced. Efforts were made to improve labor–management relations by removing bureaucratic constraints that had been imposed by the previous conglomerate's headquarters. Tight inventory controls were implemented, cutting holding costs by as much as one-half."

CHAPTER 6

"We Don't Shoot Paper at the Enemy"

ADMIRAL JOSEPH METCALF had this to say to *Newsweek* in May 1987 about the twenty tons of paper and file cabinets carried aboard the Navy's new frigates: "I find it mind-boggling. We don't shoot paper at the enemy."

We no longer measure the flood of paper in terms of the number of pages or even file boxes. Now it can be measured in tons. In a recent lawsuit brought against IBM, the prosecutors requested that IBM provide all the documents relating to the matter. What they got were four tractor-trailers filled to the roof, a sure way to frustrate and immobilize the people who brought the case. To speak of such a volume of paper as information is of course ridiculous. The kind of paper flood that is generated in many companies goes far beyond information, circles back to become mind-clogging, and finally becomes impossible for human beings to encompass. The one way to slow down paper output is to weigh the paper that comes into the IN box each day. For managers and their echelons of top staff people, pounds per week can be astounding. The briefcases of management people have grown larger and larger year by year and some of the busiest executives have switched to those bigger legal document carrying cases. As president of the University of Cincinnati, Warren Bennis, observed in the book *The Leadership Challenge* by J. Kouzes and B. Posner:

> My moment of truth came toward the end of my first ten months. It was one of those nights in the office. The clock was moving toward four in the morning, and I was still not through with the incredible mass of paper stacked before me. I was bone weary and soul weary, and I found myself muttering, "Either I can't manage this place, or it's unmanageable."

Complaining about bureaucracy and the paper mill has been an office sport for years. But now bureaucratic paper has become a significant block to growth and profits in many companies.

But the problems are not easy to resolve. For one thing, how does a management that created a bureaucratic paper glut kill it or just retard it?

Ross Perot bluntly states his position, "Written reports stifle creativity." He actually believes in operating totally without memos. So did Napoleon, who tossed out all written reports from his generals without reading them. He knew that he had already heard the

4. *In the emerging management revolution, cleaning up the headquarters bureaucracy is a top priority.*

important news. He relied on personal contact with his generals. If he had to go to the front, he went.

Smart managers are doing the same thing. If you go out there and find it out firsthand, you don't need memos, reports and other forms of chewed-over information. Paper dissolves when you close the gap between the action and the managers.

But computers are creating new morasses. Sophisticated programmers and information technologists keep presenting headquarters managers with more and more material, cross-referenced and extended, by model, size, price, color, gross margin and customer. In fact, the burgeoning new field of Management Information Systems (MIS), whatever its intent, has the effect of keeping executives away from reality. Many truly believe that they can find out all they need to know about their companies by punching up numbers on a screen every morning.

Financial reports typically cover last year and the year before by week, by month and cumulatively. All of this information can be useful, but the problem is that once the reports have been amended and refined and polished to make them shine for the brass, there is often too much volume and not enough real knowledge.

People who wear hearing aids know very well what this means. Unlike the human ear, a hearing aid has no capacity to shut out any form of sound. So, despite the remarkable benefit the device provides, it tends to wear out the user because every sound from every source comes in with the same intensity. The conversation at the next table in a restaurant can be equal in intensity to that at the table of the wearer.

In much the same way, despite the computer's enormous but undifferentiated capacity, the machine is incapable of sorting out and focusing on those facts that are of genuine significance.

If computer output is a major source of the flood, it has its equal in the internal memos that fill the corporate IN boxes. Here are the basic principles of standard business memo writing: First, of course, there is usually a need to inform specific people about something of importance. Second, there is the need to advise certain other people about the good job that is being done by the sender. Third, there is the need to let some people in power, who don't need or want the memo, be advised for purely political reasons. As an example, I saw a memo about a brilliant new idea for a *possible new product* by the project leader in a corporation's Product Development Department. Appropriately, it ended up in the IN boxes of all the people in Product Development and Market Research. But it also was sent to Public Relations, Marketing, Promotion, Advertising, Sales, Plant Production, Transportation and Legal. These additional copies were sent to further the reputation of the project leader as a bright product developer. Obviously, this type of communication was premature. Much more work needed to be done on the proposed product.

Consequently, the memo was nothing more than

added clutter, a bother to most recipients. But if the writer is bold and ambitious enough, the memo on this *possible new product* idea could end up on the chairman's desk. A huge staff obviously creates the climate that produces this memo flood aimed not only at improving the business but also at personal political objectives that have nothing to do with the efficiency of the enterprise.

John Steinbeck said that his first step in writing a novel was to write a one-page statement describing what the book would be about. He felt that if he could not get it on one page and make it clear, then the project should stop right there. Hemingway used a similar approach at the start of each book. Unfortunately this approach has not reached most companies. But as two hundred-page investment proposals flounder because of their sheer volume, growth itself begins to suffer. What is necessary is a two- or three-page investment proposal that cuts right to the key points in the purpose, the costs, and the benefits.

The information glut is dramatically illustrated in the area of scientific publications. There are more than eight thousand scientific articles published each day. Scientific and technical information increases about 15 percent each year. This means that it doubles in five years. At that rate, it will increase even faster in the future. Then even the most dedicated readers will not be able to get through all the relevant material.

Tom Peters, who has done much to discover, describe and stimulate change, has this to say to those who attend his seminars, "When you get back to work, check your IN box. Measure it, quantitatively. How many papers, or pages, deal with internal affairs such as the minutes of committee meetings or personnel actions? And how many deal directly with customer-survey results, complaints (or compliments) and correspondence? Of your 'closely watched' numbers (the half-dozen litmus test indicators that almost all effective managers seem able to recall from memory), how many are customer-centered?"

The key measure in this evaluation of the paper flood is to sort out the amount of internal paper that circulates among staff people and the amount that is external and relates specifically to the customer and markets. All too often the weight of internal paper outweighs the external. And there is the problem defined.

How serious is this paper flood problem? Read all of the paper for just a single month: the sales reports, the financial reports, the production reports, the publicity, the advertising, the promotion, legal agreements, internal memos, field reports, quality control reports, trade papers. Then see if you have time for anything else.

At the Pall Corp., a leading filter producer, Abe Krasnoff, the president, rarely uses the traditional typed memo. Sometimes he passes on longhand notes. Krasnoff believes that when he has something of significance to say, he should go out and meet the man or woman and say it in person. Krasnoff meets, he telephones, he talks to groups, he carries his message to the point where the action desired takes place. He moves around the company and around the market and with his customers to deliver his message personally. And equally important, he asks questions and listens. Krasnoff's style is relaxed and positive, and he is able to get an exchange of information that is invaluable. He finds out firsthand what is right and what is wrong about the company. In his company he never lets the paper mill even begin to run.

Building computer reports from the front line is the most effective way to gather and present truly useful information, especially about markets, sales and competitors.

Without such planning from the ground up, computers can produce a data flood that can be overwhelming to the point of being useless. The total of all the sales areas reports, when combined in a single batch for the vice-president of sales, may be measured in pounds, not in pages. This situation has produced the need for programmers to repeat the process they use in working with the field sales people and do the same thing all over again to determine what kind of report will be useful and efficient for the top man in sales. Too often, sales reports from the computer are four inches thick. One a month produces a stack of reports about four feet high by the end of the year. Such reports could not exist if they had to be produced manually.

There are wide variations in the way reports are used at different levels within the organization. Field sales people need one form of report, the sales manager needs another. And so on.

Computer programmers are being pushed out to the

5. *A week in the market with field sales people will certainly make the programmer's output more effective.*

Frank A. Armstrong

front line to see and learn what is being done and how
it is being done and in the process they are producing
programs and reports that are becoming more and
more useful. A week in the plant or in the field does
wonders for the folks who devise the programs that
produce the reports.

CHAPTER 7

New-Style Managers Are Managing from the Marketplace

EXECUTIVES WHO go into the field and run their businesses from the midst of the action find that the marketplace loses its complexity. It becomes easier to analyze and to sell.

Roger Penske, the one-time racing car driver and brilliant entrepreneur, acquired Detroit Diesel Corp. from General Motors in 1987. It had been a big loser for GM, enmeshed as it was in the dense web of the corporation's monstrous bureaucracy. From the moment Penske took over, he has stressed close personal contact with the operators of diesel-powered trucks, boats, generators and construction equipment, not just with the companies that buy the engines and build the equipment but with the truck owners, boat captains, power engineers and contractors who actually use them.

Penske himself goes to see the customers every chance he gets. Since his arrival on the scene, Detroit Diesel managers have come to expect to field late-night phone queries or complaints from truck fleet owners and to dispatch parts by private plane, if necessary, to keep a truck on the road. Penske is a driven leader who seeks customer satisfaction in every possible way. In the last year, Penske invited more than twenty-five hundred customers and vendors to tour the Detroit Diesel factory in the Detroit suburb of Redford to observe the changes and preview new products of Detroit Diesel. Penske also invited the Detroit Diesel work force to the Marlboro 500 race at Michigan International Speedway in Brooklyn, Michigan, which his company owns.

Penske has also striven to reduce the tensions between former GM hourly workers represented by the United Auto Workers and management supervisors. "We had twelve hundred grievances when we took over Detroit Diesel and a year later we had forty-four outstanding," he said. "My goal is to not have any."

"Everybody talks about team effort, but it's got to start at the top," said James Brown, shop chairman of UAW local 163. "Penske has the ability to reach out to people. That's so important. We've got the best engine builders in the world in this plant, and they've never had a chance to talk to someone who would listen to them. Under GM, this place wasn't going to last very long. Now we see a great future."

Let's face it: There has to be someplace for record keeping, information disbursement and financial con-

6.   *No man's knowledge can go beyond his personal experience.*
—John Locke

trol. But it is possible to lead a business from the field and from regional offices or simply from wherever you happen to be in the market. Lately regional offices are being given most of the authority needed to run their segments of the business.

IBM has recently divided and separated its business into four operating units, recognizing that the complexity of its various markets and the inherent differences in these markets require such a separation.

One of the most acute problems American corporations face is the unwillingness of top executives to listen to criticism. Managers become isolated, surrounded by people trained to agree. Executives hear only the things their people think they want to hear. And if they don't get out into the field, that is all they ever know. That syndrome is extremely dangerous, as management people are discovering.

I once asked Stuart Watson, then chairman of Heublein, about his company's initial inability to manage its Kentucky Fried Chicken fast-food acquisition effectively. He said that the problem grew out of Heublein's experience in the wine and liquor business. There it didn't seem to matter what a retail liquor outlet looked like. Heublein's Smirnoff vodka didn't get the blame if the floor was dirty. After all, the vodka was produced at the distillery and put into a sealed bottle. And that, according to Watson, was how it was viewed by consumers even if they bought the bottle in a pigpen.

But with fast food manufactured at the retail premises, the story was totally different: Consumers cared a lot about the looks and the sanitation of the premises where their food was cooked and sold. But it took Heublein a while to figure that out; that is, to understand that with its acquisition of Kentucky Fried, it had bought what amounted to five thousand little fried chicken factories all over the world.

To handle that business properly, Heublein had to add an entirely new discipline to its organization. It had to manage precisely what was going on at the point of sale. That meant the company had to train staff, inspect the premises, correct errors and improve the quality of the product in every retail outlet, in sharp contrast to its laissez faire attitude toward liquor retailers.

A leading exponent of the need for management involvement in the marketplace was United Airlines' Ed Carlson, who said, "I traveled about two hundred thousand miles a year to express my concern for what I call visible management. I often used to say to Mrs. Carlson when I'd come home for a weekend that I felt as though I were running for public office. I'd get off an airplane, I'd shake hands with any United employees I could find."

Campbell Soup reorganized into fifty-two business units to speed product development and market creation. The change worked: product development increased. The new $300 million Canadian unit, for example, introduced a new and quite different formulation of V-8 Juice for French-speaking Canadians. It hadn't occurred to anybody at U.S. headquarters that French Canadians' taste in tomatoes might be different from that of their English-speaking counterparts. But it was, and the special new product was a big success.

Allen Mebane, top manager of Unifi, a producer of textured polyester yarn, says, "I have got to know my customer's business and problems as well as I know my own. If I can't show him how much I can help him, I won't keep his business for long." Mebane emphasizes the importance of getting inside the customer's mind and of the personal identification of management with this overriding value.

Frito-Lay has long maintained a big lead in the snack-food business. It sends out more than nine thousand route sales people each day. And despite its commanding lead in market share, Frito-Lay has taken steps to increase its contacts with its customers. Marketing staff members, once located in the Dallas headquarters, have been reassigned to eight regional offices in an effort to base brand strategy at the marketplace rather than the home office. The share of the marketing budget for local needs has risen dramatically. Frito-Lay's director of field marketing declares, "There's no such thing as a national program for promotions coming out of Frito-Lay anymore. We will tailor our marketing to our prime trading areas. We are tailoring our program to meet the needs of individual chains."

J. Willard Marriott Sr., past eighty years old, was still worrying about the cleanliness of a single hotel's lobby. Marriott, Ray Kroc of McDonald's, Bill Hewlett and David Packard of Hewlett-Packard, James C. Penney, Robert Wood Johnson of Johnson & Johnson and Ed Carlson of United Airlines were all deeply committed

7. *Smart managers know that they earn money for their companies by making money for their customers.*

to their customers, to granting autonomy to their executives, and most of all to the significance of knowledge of the marketplace, the front line.

In contrast, I've been on trips to the market with automobile industry executives who have no understanding of what is going on in their markets and don't seem to know how to find out. They go in force and meet dealers in groups at formal gatherings, presumably to listen. But dealers who valued their franchises would not say what they thought if it would jeopardize their status. Yet top executives honestly believe they are in contact with the market, with their customers. Attending local auto shows provides still more of the appearance of being in touch without any reality.

Astute executives have always known that dealers and sales people are not dumb. And now a lot more executives know that they can learn useful, even crucial information from their sales people, distributors and customers.

If the home-office mentality is no longer to dominate management thinking, where do executives work when they are at home? The trick is not to attach any special status to headquarters. Any office should serve without any display of rank. Everything at headquarters should restate the idea that the marketplace is where we do business and where we go to understand how to do it better.

Locked in his office, the leader's visibility to people in the marketplace is reduced to the printed word, usually in the trade press. But media coverage rarely brings to the market and to the customer a message that influ-

8.
If you know more about the marketplace than your competitors know, you are bound to win.

ences company performance. When management goes to the marketplace with enough consistency to become an important, visible factor, the impact in a particular market is immediate and memorable.

The turnaround of Chrysler, the refinancing of the business and the return to sales growth and profit of the company was, in large part, achieved by the most visible man in American business, Lee Iacocca. The decision to use him in advertising as the spokesman for the company's products was an obvious and smart choice. He has been a believable and effective salesman. This is an extreme example of visibility and the power of such visibility in the marketplace. But this technique is not for many companies or for many company leaders. Chrysler was in a unique situation. The same approach, using the company leader as the television spokesman, has become almost a fad, and most times the result is undistinguished.

Ernest Gallo's retailers and distributors do not soon forget a visit by the vintner. I admire the way he operates. He has built the company into the most powerful in the wine industry. One of the factors that created that dominance is the way Ernest Gallo handles problems in a market when sales begin to slide. If that was happening in Houston, for example, Ernest would call the distributor and tell him he was coming to see him. When? "Tomorrow afternoon." Gallo would leave at once for Houston and spend that afternoon and evening and the next morning in retail stores seeing and hearing how Gallo and the distributor were doing. He would talk to everyone, taking notes at every stop. By the time of his scheduled meeting with the distributor, he would have a list of specific actions that he wanted the distributor to take to get Gallo's market share "up where it belongs." This was, in most cases, a one-way conversation. Gallo had already seen and talked to enough retailers to know what had to be done to turn the tide in Houston. Gallo did the same thing in fifty or more markets, so he knew exactly what he was doing wherever he went. As a result, the failings in a particular market were easily identified, and he and the distributor knew what to do about them.

A program of visible market contacts takes time to build into a significant force. Long hours, lots of miles and tons of patience are factors that all will be rewarded with dividends in time. A build-up of impressions among people in the market becomes a significant and measurable force.

This is not to deny the fundamental reason for going to the market in the first place: to give the marketplace the opportunity for precise communication about the company, the products, the competition, the service, the distribution, the pricing—all of which can influence major decisions by the company.

At the same time, the visibility of management in the market improves the entire image of the company. This can have a direct positive effect on sales. In a totally different field, David Ogilvy, the renowned advertising man, makes much the same point: "Do not summon people to your office. Instead go to see them in their offices. This makes you visible throughout the company. A chairman who never wanders about his agency becomes a hermit, out of touch with his staff."

People in the marketplace will come to realize that the company really wants to know what is going on in their market. The company, they come to understand, "really cares what I think."

Compare the impact on the marketplace of visible management to what can be achieved through press stories and annual reports. All this printed communication joins the flood that hits the marketplace from the industry. It is piled high in stacks on customers' desks. Sometimes it gets a quick glance, but more often than not it is simply lost in the shuffle. Visible management, simply by its presence, tells the market many things about the company that truly can't be communicated effectively and forcefully in any other way. Visible management tells the market:

"We are aggressive."

"We come seeking information."

"We want to improve what we do."

"We are open to new ideas."

"We are ready to change."

"We need your help."

"We do what others do not do."

"We want to be the best."

CHAPTER 8

The Most Important Questions About a Business Are Those That Penetrate to the Real World of the Customer

WHAT MANAGEMENT people think they know about a customer or a competitor may be more wrong than right. There is great temptation to overestimate the validity of past experience. But one person really does know: the customer. Only by asking the customers, by watching them, by trying to understand their behavior can you find out how they buy, how they use what they buy, what they expect, what they value.

Business is a process that converts this knowledge into economic power in the marketplace. It gives a business a leadership position on which success and survival depend. Executives of high-growth companies generally spend substantially more time with their customers than do their counterparts in mature business corporations. On average, according to one recent study, leaders of middle-sized high-growth companies spend roughly half of their time working directly with their customers. That is because they know that you can't accept a statement as true simply because it used to be true. Things change. It must never be assumed that something has not been altered by the passage of time, by changing tastes, new needs. So the questions executives ask must try to fathom the circumstances now, see what has changed, determine how the change affects what is being offered.

I ran a test market in Rochester, New York, on a new vitamin-enriched juice drink called Drink 10. It had been a success in West Germany. All the chain stores in the Rochester area stocked the product, and the test was backed by television advertising. I got the usual reports from the market on case sales per store, special promotions, and so on. Then I went to Rochester to see for myself. Samples of the product were being offered in stores, and I watched and listened to the reactions of customers. They liked the taste. They liked the idea of the extra vitamins the product featured. They thought the package was attractive. But when they heard the price for twenty-eight ounces, nine out of ten of them thought it was too high. This was the case in five of the stores I checked during the samplings. The product was too good, too expensive, even for an upscale market like Rochester. A price cut of thirty cents might have worked, but that would have all but eliminated profit. So the result of the market test was not to market Drink 10 in the U.S.

The function of such work is not to prove a point, but

to test it. Its object is to keep open all possibilities other than a preconceived one and to expose the mind of the executive to a huge number of other previously unseen possibilities. Certainly the purpose is not to develop an emotional attachment to an opinion the marketplace rejects.

Sometimes what a company thinks is the most important feature of a product, something perceived at headquarters as its "quality," may be unimportant to the customer. The right knowledge is what is needed to exploit the market opportunities. Does the business have the knowledge needed to give it leadership in the market?

Anyone who sits in business conferences knows that far too often the emphasis is on agreeing on something, rather than on tearing it apart to find out what is true. Over a long time, Dr. Irving J. Lee of the Northwestern University business school worked with a variety of businesses as a consultant on matters of internal and external communications. As a result, he sat in on two hundred staff, board and committee meetings over an extended period.

Lee reported the results in his article "Why Discussions Go Astray," which was published in the book *Language, Meaning and Maturity* by S. I. Hayakawa. Describing these experiences, Lee wrote: "Far too much time is spent considering proposals to correct problems that were not accurately defined." He found much time and energy was spent presenting and listening to solutions, which, once the problems were analyzed, were found to have nothing to do with them.

9. Find out what customers buy from others and why.

They may have been solutions, but not to the real problems. Some managers became solution-minded before they know the realities of the marketplace.

No hard and fast rule can be used to determine the key factor in a marketplace. From the start, one needs to adopt an "intelligently ignorant" stance. Many experienced managers often try to use *yesterday*'s facts to achieve *today*'s objectives. It must seem pointless to go out to the marketplace when so much is available in written reports and in committee meetings. But that is almost always out-of-date, second-hand stuff. And if they don't go to the marketplace themselves, they cannot understand the problems and what needs to be done about them today. The need to know the facts and to find the key factors is constant. Personal observation may be difficult, but there is no substitute.

10. *In one of his remarkably discerning epigrams, C. F. Kettering, the automotive inventor and General Motors research executive, said, "A man must have a certain amount of intelligent ignorance to get anywhere."*

CHAPTER 9

The Top People Have to be Out Working With Customers

ONE OF the most important aspects of going into the marketplace is that you can't delegate it. You have to go yourself. Here are the kind of comments I have heard from people who are leading major businesses now and think they are in touch with their customers:

- "My style always has been hands-on. All the office work and paperwork has to be done, but I like to stay close to the market, talk on the phone to every regional manager every week and take every call from important customers at any time." (Auto parts)
- "I try to stay close to the market. It's not easy. Our shares in Cincinnati and Salt Lake and Phoenix and Boston are up for this last period, but we're losing in Chicago, Minneapolis, Oshkosh and Indi-

anapolis. That midwest region is beginning to worry me. We lost share overall last year, but I'm tracking it closely." (A marketing director in soap)

- "I started on the street in Des Moines. I'll never forget my first year on a sales route. I don't get out as much as I would like to now, but I still stay in touch with the market. Only last week when I was in Des Moines . . ." (Sales manager in paper products)
- "I have every major competitive model in my house, nine of them. I like to see how they perform against our newest models. I project to the consumer, I see what they see. See what they like. It's a rather simple method and for me, it works." (Television)
- "You know this is one tough business. The whole thing starts all over every season. I have my girls constantly shopping every competitor. Not only here. But in Los Angeles, Dallas and Miami. A bit tricky, but we get it done. In this business you stay close to the customer, or you drop dead." (Fashion)

All of these people firmly believe in the fundamental truth that it is essential to stay close to the market, close to the customer, close to the competition. But none of them does it, even though they think they do. They rarely get out. They talk about being "hands-on," about being close to the market, but as you read their comments you see that what they are doing is not close to the customer but close to the office. They are working with paper and long-distance telephone contact and talk with their staff people about the market, customers, competitors, problems. They are not directly and personally involved with day-to-day action in the plant, in the marketplace.

The time has come to restore the original meaning to a phrase that has been misused for so long and for management to become truly "hands-on."

The filtering and interpretation done by managers who are not truly "hands-on" creates potential distortion. They produce what their people think is "what they want to hear." This is the major problem in American business today as it has always been with bureaucratic organizations, only more so because of modern reporting and computer systems. The tendency to stay comfortably at home is a natural and a destructive one.

Here is a mail survey taken by L. Shoemaker & Co., an Atlanta-based management and consulting company, among 310 top managers in a cross-section of American business. Top executives were surveyed because what they do inevitably affects the rest of the organization. What they do will certainly define how finance, marketing, sales and production managers approach their jobs. Industries covered included airlines, aluminum, appliances, automobiles, beverages, boats, computers, cosmetics, fashion, food, furniture, liquor, men's clothing, oil, shoes, steel, supermarket retailing, telecommunications. The survey covered representative companies selling products and services through every means available to reach the ultimate consumer. The survey did not directly approach the subject of management style or method. Instead it was simply a measure of how the executives spend their time managing their businesses. The study accounted for all the time that each executive spent at work during a typical four-week period. That period was chosen to give the figures balance. Here is the weekly average. No consideration was given to vacation or travel time.

Activity	Weekly hours
Creating and consuming paperwork	20
Staff meetings	15
Committee reports	5
Conventions, trade meetings	2
Public service	2
Out with customers, salespeople, etc.	4
Miscellaneous	12
Total weekly hours	60

As you would expect, the top managers work hard, spending long hours at the job. But they are not paid just to work long hours. They are there to get results, and too many of them are spending far too much time "tending the store" and not tending to the market, to customers, to plants and to competitors. Too much time is spent in the office making sure the office runs well. Too much time is spent in meetings with staff people. Far too many projects are given to committees to work on and to "report back on." Going to conventions and trade meetings is, at best, the softest form of keeping in touch with the business. The same applies to an occasional one-hour plant tour. Public service is fine as long as it is kept to a reasonable minimum. There's no point in a CEO trying to help the city while his company grows soft. This will not benefit the community nearly so much as a company's strong sales and profit.

I believe many managers simply do not spend enough time finding out the truth about how their business is doing, about how the plant is running at the production floor, about how competitive products stack up against their own, about how the salespeople are functioning in the market, about what customers think about their contacts with the company and its products.

The new market driven style of management has been described by René McPherson, chairman of the Dana Corp. He says: "Until we believe that the expert in any particular job is most often the person performing it, we shall forever limit the potential of that person in terms of both his contribution to the organization and his personal development. Nobody knows more about how to operate a machine, maximize its output, improve its quality, optimize the material flow, and keep it operating efficiently than does the machine operator."

Some executives in the auto industry have finally learned this. That is why many Ford Motor senior plant managers have shut down their offices and moved their desks down to the factory floor.

I have worked with Rose Marie Reed, who built a highly successful women's swimsuit business. She did it by dividing her work time between two places. Half her time was spent in workrooms seeing to it that the fabrics and the sewing and construction were right. She would often sit at a machine and do the job herself to see if it could be done and how to do it right. The rest of the time she worked in the marketplace, in the stores with such customers as Saks Fifth Avenue, I. Magnin, J.L. Hudson, Rich's, and Neiman Marcus, among others. She worked on the sales floor talking to customers, helping them select and fit swimsuits. She listened to what they had to say. She learned firsthand what they liked and didn't like. And she carried this knowledge back to her design group and to her workrooms to guide the creation of next season's Rose Marie Reed line. The character of the business was created by the character and methods of Rose Marie Reed. But when the business was sold to a large apparel manufacturer, its character was submerged in that of the larger company. The business declined over time. It lost the invaluable involvement that had been provided by Rose Marie in the workrooms, in stores and with customers.

From the field of literature comes author John le Carré who, in a comment he made during a 1988 BBC television broadcast, put a button on the whole matter: "A desk is a dangerous place from which to view the world." He was talking about his philosophy of writing and the sources of his material and inspiration.

11. *The days of the "potted plant" manager are over. The job of going out to your market, to customers and to competitors can't be delegated.*

CHAPTER *10*

See the Market for Yourself: There is no Short Cut

SAM WALTON may never have heard of the philosopher John Locke or his remarkably perceptive observation that "no man's knowledge can go beyond his personal experience." But few business executives understand and profit from that idea better than Walton, one of the most successful retailers in history. The creator of the $15 billion Wal-Mart retailing chain, he has never used an office for anything more than a place to pick up his mail. He has built and run Wal-Mart by being where his business happens. Walton spends just about all his time in his stores or in his competitors'. He knows just about all he needs to know about his business simply by being out there where the business is being done.

Walton knows what is selling and what is not. He knows why. He knows from clerks, from checkout cashiers, from warehouse people. He knows from his managers, too. But most important, Sam Walton knows from the sales floor up all that he needs to know about Wal-Mart.

He talks. He asks. But mostly he listens. Not in meetings but one-to-one. Walton wants to hear what everyone in his business has to say about what they are doing and how they are doing it, what they like, and what they don't like.

In the small town of Starkville, Mississippi, a new Wal-Mart store stands on a high hill just outside of town. I went into this clean, brightly lit, fully stocked store and asked clerks for help on five different items.

They not only had the answers to my questions but they guided me to the products with apparently genuine interest. They clearly reflected Wal-Mart's attitude: We're here to help you any way we can.

Walton's method of gaining information about how his business works reflects an indispensable need throughout business to meet and know all the people in the entire chain of production and distribution who touch a product or service from origin to ultimate user. All of them know things that can be useful.

It is vital to meet the people in the company who represent the front line of the organization on a one-to-one basis and to know what they do and to know how they do it. When they know that this is the way their company is being managed, whatever their position, they will be eager to talk and to help.

Clearly this is not the way the typical CEO works, even in an industry as market-oriented as retailing.

This is managing in a radically different form and place: It is management away from the office. But it is management nevertheless, because it involves thinking about the business in the midst of a multitude of stimuli that present realities that executives at headquarters rarely face. That is quite different from thinking about the business in the home office or thinking about the business among staff people or thinking about the business at meetings or thinking about the business while reading reports. It is different from thinking about the people who cannot know firsthand what is happening and why, because they are not there.

This is managing in the most stimulating environment possible. Every contact will produce information about the business. A ten-hour day out in the market with people at all levels will produce hours of useful information about the business. More and more management people believe totally in this new method of front-line leadership.

In the past, recalls recruiter William Battolia, companies looked for executives who could delegate responsibility and then coach, cajole or threaten their people to get the job done, but not anymore. Nowadays, says Joseph DiMario, an executive vice-president of Mellon Bank, "Managers have got to get their hands dirty."

Dennis Marini of Harris Corp. concurs: "Managers have got to do more just like their people on the line." Downsizing has propelled the change. "With fewer managers, executives can't just delegate and stand

12. *Manage at the place where the business happens and with the people who make it happen.*

back supervising people doing their thing," explains Paul Kerins, an executive vice-president of Barnett Banks.

Michael Haverty, a vice-president of the Atchison, Topeka & Santa Fe railway, argues that today's business environment is "too fast and competitive" for managers to sit back and run the business from the home office. Centralized structures are changing all across America. In business, new leaders are rebuilding America from the bottom up into a stronger and more balanced industrial society.

Some years ago, when I began handling the advertising agency account for Coca-Cola, I concluded that I needed to know more about the business than I was learning from reading reports and talking to my agency associates in New York. I went to various markets and met with Coke field men and bottlers. I quickly discovered that there was a great difference in Coke marketing and sales, market by market, and in particular in southern versus northern markets. What Coke needed in Chicago, Detroit, Philadelphia and Cleveland was a quite different matter from what the product needed in New Orleans, Houston, Dallas and Atlanta. In the north it was a struggle to grow at all, while in the south it was simply a matter of "how high do we want to go?" In recent years much has changed, but the dramatic difference in market shares and people's abilities and attitudes by market has never left my mind.

How much time should the CEO spend in the market? A better way to ask this question is how much time should management spend actually managing the business?

The typical CEO, however well-intentioned, becomes immersed in the trappings of office, protected from reality by one or two secretaries, by staff people determined not to be the bearers of bad news (no matter how significant to the future of the enterprise), and by endless meetings. When he does go into the field, he moves by private jet and limousine in an entourage whose members and schedule are prepared far in advance so that every semblance of reality can be expunged and only a bright and shining vision of his colonies will be seen—a kind of Potemkin village. And yet this style (it should not be called a method) is what executives strive to reach. It is the usual reward for a life of diligence, astute politics and business skill. It is the way the top executive operates in most companies.

But it is emphatically not the way executives with an awareness of the increasingly competitive nature of business today run a company. No innovator, no CEO with a sense of the force of change runs his business this way. Sam Walton is certainly not the only CEO who manages the way he does, with both feet firmly planted in contemporary reality.

But it is a style of management that won't go away quickly. Getting rid of the superficial aspects of leadership is not an easy matter. The importance of the trappings of power can't be easily dismissed. The appeal to ego cannot be denied. These things are, after all, what make a lot of executives feel good about themselves and their companies, from which they derive much of their positive energy.

Since the mid-1980s, however, this whole approach to management has begun to be questioned seriously by many observers and practitioners. The way to effect necessary changes is a demanding one. The leaders must get out of the office, get away from the whole idea that the home office is where the business begins and ends. It does not in either a practical or in a theoretical way. Only when top management takes off, goes to the marketplace, works in the marketplace and leads from the marketplace, can change take place. With that major reorientation, everything else needed to make the business more competitive and aggressive and effective will follow almost automatically.

The best companies today learn from the people they serve. They provide unparalleled quality, service and reliability. They succeed by being customer-oriented. Maytag and Frito-Lay are classic examples. IBM's marketing vice-president, Francis G. (Buck) Rogers, said, "It's a shame that in so many companies whenever you give customers special service, it's an exception." Not so with the best companies. Everyone gets into the act. Many of the innovative companies got their best product ideas from customers. That comes from listening, intently and regularly.

What all of this suggests is that the organizational chart almost literally must be turned upside down. Nordstrom, the big West Coast retailer now moving into the east, has done it. Top management's role is to support the front-line people. Middle management's role is to act largely as facilitator, speeding up actions. Middle management is no longer the umpire in charge of constraining, preventing or slowing action in the name of rights or integrity.

Take all the evidence together, and a clear picture of the successful company in the 1990s emerges. It will be flatter because it will have fewer layers of organizational structure, and it will have more autonomous units, more local authority, with fewer central-staff second-guessers.

James Jones in his novel *The Thin Red Line* describes a situation in battle that dramatizes the old way of doing things. First there are the painful details about what the men in a particular platoon are going through during a firefight in the front line. Men are being hit and killed, some are frozen in terror. They can see the difference between what has been ordered from the rear, what should be done and what actually can be done at the front.

The scene then shifts to battalion headquarters about a mile to the rear. What the major thinks is going on in the front line and what is actually going on are quite different. Orders are based on what he *thinks* the situation is, based on his secondhand information. The scene then shifts back another two miles to division headquarters, where the general is giving orders with even less accurate information, but with even more impact than the major. War is hell, but it is worse than that when the front-line soldier is the only guy who truly understands how it is being run.

The most effective leaders, from Gandhi to Sam Walton of Wal-Mart, have always led from the front. Today, any leader at any level who hopes for even limited success must lead from the market. The need for change is first discovered where the customer is, where the mall is, where the innovative competitor is emerging, where the angry dealer is and not far away in the isolated calm of a conference room at headquarters.

Fred Turner, McDonald's chairman, started out as a shoe salesman. That is where he learned what it was to get the basics right, to know customers and take pride in and responsibility for the job. Turner says, "History shows that our competition's involvement doesn't last. They just don't have the depth of attention to detail."

McDonald's believes that senior managers should be in the field, paying attention to employees, training and execution. McDonald's founder Ray Kroc said, "I believe that less is more in the case of corporate management; for its size, McDonald's is the most unstructured corporation I know, and I don't think you could find a happier, more secure, harder working group of executives anywhere."

Kroc stated in the book *In Search of Excellence* by Tom Peters and Robert Waterman, "A well-run restaurant is like a winning baseball team. It makes the most of every crew member's talent and takes advantage of every split-second opportunity to speed up service." Kroc focused on the little things: "I emphasize the importance of details. You must perfect every fundamental of your business if you expect it to perform well." Getting the details right, McDonald's way, requires an astonishing amount of learning and inten-

13. *Managers in the field become magnets for enormously valuable information.*

sity. Says a former employee, "When I first started, they put a little white hat on me that said 'trainee.' They started me right off in the easiest of jobs—cooking french fries. Then I moved from fries to shakes. So it went, on up to handling the buns and cooking the burgers."

Work in the market by the top management group can't be delegated. When they are in the market they see what others do not see. Managers will, by the very fact that they are out there getting ideas and advice from people in the market, get what others will not get. Those who manage from the field will see and learn things that others miss, because they come to the market with awareness that this is a vital mission. What they see and learn and decide can make a difference in how the business performs. And all of the details that they absorb will help them gain the insights that can be important in making crucial decisions on products, people, marketing and planning.

Consider the plight of the old-style leader. Consider what he is missing. Consider the quality of his information as it comes to him filtered and condensed in reports from the field and from staff members.

An example of this came to me in my years in the vitamin business. I visited a large health food store on Wabash Avenue in Chicago. The owner liked to talk about the business. I listened and asked what was selling and what wasn't selling. He picked up a box that contained small packets of vitamin pills. He said, "Here's a good idea. All they need in one packet each day. But it has been a bomb. Hasn't sold. They backed

Frank A. Armstrong

it with a big splashy two-page ad in color. Nothing. I think the reason is the whole idea isn't clear. The box doesn't explain it. Nor the name. But I still think the basic idea is good." And he was right. With better packaging design, better package communication, that package became the leading seller for my Rich Life brand of health foods.

Going to the market provides the best and most visible measure of the commitment of management to leading the business. There is no show of power here, no symbols or trappings. Instead there is a strong message that the intent is to do the best job possible. There is clear reason for others to follow. This new style of leadership can transform any business, because top management people are working for all of the people in the market and in the company, not just for themselves. The people on the front line become people with names, abilities, and achievements. They are no longer all alone out there. They have allies, and they know that the most important management people in the company want to know how to better the company for all of them.

The future of a business does not come in a sudden rush of inspiration, nor does it come in a single brilliant idea. It comes slowly in thousands of pieces of information from hundreds of sources. It comes from what is seen, from what is heard, from what is touched and from what is compared. It comes from negative as well as positive comments. It comes from the whole market, in a sense from the whole world out there.

With personal knowledge of the market, managers

14. *Know what is wrong with your products.*

will in fact be able to see more clearly not only where the business is today in real time, but even more important, they will be able to see more closely and accurately where the business is going.

In the market, the new leaders are visible. Their people see them. They know they are out there. Competitors know that they are out there and have to be concerned, especially if their own management is sitting back in the home office reading reports and working with the staff, far from where real business is being done.

Ted Santo, a senior manager at Dayton Power & Light, said in *Thriving on Chaos* by Tom Peters: "My office is indeed gone. I wanted to wait a while before describing the effects so I could be sure of my feelings and to be sure my feelings wouldn't change over time. It has been seven months now and I still don't miss it. I love the 'freedom' it has given me to move about or wander. I find myself meeting people more often and on their turf. As luck would have it, I have been promoted recently and have gained the responsibility for three new departments. Fortunately, without a large stuffy office, I have the freedom to jump around all four work areas. My former office would have been even more of a hindrance to me now then it was before."

Management has to go out to the market to avoid the distortion of vital information. When information comes in after traveling up through three or four levels, distortion is likely. In a small business with twenty salesmen, this happens. In an office with only ten people, this happens. People don't like to bring bad news to the top. This is particularly true of sales organizations. They want every report to be upbeat. That is the nature of people in sales.

The philosopher Vilfredo Pareto has written, "Logic is useful for proof, but almost never for making discoveries." The planned "state visit" by management can be fashioned by subordinates to ensure that the views they've espoused to the boss won't be distorted by, say, an irate customer.

The distortion of information is everywhere. It is worse in Washington than in Des Moines. But not by much. Distortion in the large company can be mind-boggling. People unintentionally shade the truth. Three or four little shadings in sequence can destroy reality completely.

Getting out and about is the big idea. But it is more than that. It is an attitude toward managing and leading. It deals with the fundamental way in which communication takes place in gathering the information necessary for decision making.

Psychologist and philosopher William James, writing in 1890 in his renowned book, *Pragmatism*, stated the case for habit in a smoothly functioning society, but also drew a bleak picture of the entrapment and despair that can result:

Habit is thus the enormous flywheel of society, its most precious conservative agent. It alone is what keeps us all within the bounds of ordinance, and saves the children of fortune from the envious uprisings of the poor. It alone prevents the hardest and most repulsive walks of life from being deserted by those brought up to tread therein. It keeps the fisherman and the deckhand at sea through the winter. It holds the miner in his darkness, and nails the countryman to his log cabin and his lonely farm through all the months of snow. It protects us from invasion by the natives of the desert and the frozen zone. It dooms all to fight out the battle of life upon which we are fitted and it is too late to begin again.

CHAPTER **11**

Go to the Marketplace Alone

THE MANAGER who travels alone gains much more than speed. He opens sources of information from the people in the front line, in the market, that he could never get in a group. The presence of even one or two other people changes the situation. One-to-one is clearly the most effective form of communication. The ability to ask and get honest responses increases. Information from the market is direct and without distortion or "shading." Add just one staff person or other "outsider" and the situation changes. Three people are then involved and the possibilities of distortion and misinterpretation of information increase.

IBM's Allen Krowe, head of IBM's Rochester laboratory, supports this point in an article in the New York *Times* in 1986. He says, "There's a tendency—I call it the holding-company syndrome—for managements to remove themselves, to be concerned about the big picture, about financial structure, about redeploying assets. That's anathema to my work here. We feel we better darned well understand those matters, but we will not let go of the business. When we all feel that we're getting a little out of touch on something, you'll find us on field trips out to the Rochester lab, or on trips to a branch office to meet with customers, salesmen and systems engineers, or perhaps on a trip down to Raleigh to get a briefing on our connectivity strategy."

Harry Gray, former CEO of United Technologies, began as a salesman. He says that the reason he did so well (for his Pratt & Whitney Aircraft division) against General Electric's aircraft engine division "was that I showed up in places with customers where I never saw the top management of General Electric."

Consider how different this management approach is from the home-office-bound outlook of old-style top managers who believe that they have to stay close to the office to control the business—and protect their jobs—and that if they leave for long periods, the business will begin to flounder. That is simply not the case if management changes the location for managing the business from the office to the marketplace, that is, to the front line.

Stuck in the office, the old-style manager has almost no firsthand experiences. Instead he gets "input," an enormous amount of stale information filtered through the staff organization. He forces more and more decisions to come to his desk, and he spends too much time on trivial matters that should be handled by the caretakers who are paid to keep things neat and well oiled.

But that requires more than just going out to the

market, the plant, the customers, the competition. It requires a positive view of the purpose of the work. Professor G. Allen of London University reports in an article "The British Disease" in the *Times* of London that the wrong attitude can make the effort of going out to see and learn a useless exercise: "Groups of manufacturers and workers [from England] went to America under the Anglo–American Productivity Scheme. A group of trade unionists from the iron-and-steel industry were given an opportunity to examine the highly efficient Japanese steel plants. In the course of official inquiries into [various] industries the members of the investigating body have often been taken to countries where the corresponding industry is supposed to be well conducted. But the industrial tourists, while admiring the methods of their foreign hosts, usually, on their return, bend their minds to finding reasons why foreign ways would not succeed here."

This is also reflected in a remark of Apple CEO John Sculley quoted in *Thriving on Chaos*: "Hang out at most corporate headquarters and you soon come to believe that in most firms everyone on the line is considered a 'bozo.' It is as if there aren't any dumb marketing staffers or smart sales people. It's the wrong attitude. Disrespect leads to subtle—and not so subtle—denigration when decisions are being made."

For example, fellow executives have been heard to comment about Tom Wilson, Boeing's chief executive, "He's still out in the shop," and, when the occasion arises, he still makes a few crucial design decisions.

When a manager heads out there, it is helpful to give

some, but not much, advance notice. Short notice is not meant to "catch" people; it is meant to head off the truth-inhibiting formal preparations that typically are made when managers go to the field from headquarters. It is a wasted effort if the trip to the market is done by a group of staff people, all hard at work taking notes and writing up reports at night in a motel room after a long day on the road. The whole effort is hurt by such a formal approach. Instead, one management person working alone can gain insights and information that will never surface when a group hits the road.

Lanier's chairman, Gene Milner, and its president, Wes Cantrell, think alike on this subject. Says Cantrell, "Gene and I were the only president and chairman at last year's major word-processing conference. We were pleased to see the lack of competitive management there."

Management people who started in sales and marketing in the field have an even greater need to go out to the market, back to the front line. That is because they are most likely to conclude that they have seen it all before and that there is "no need to see it again." These are not casual quotes. They are accurate statements from managers who have worked in the marketplace in the past and don't want to do it again. They have done it all and, with promotion to higher management level, they feel they don't have to do it again.

The market is changing at this very moment, as it always does. This change is rapid and continual and the rate of change is increasing month by month with the growing impact of overseas competition and more aggressive (or desperate) domestic competition.

I have seen this again and again with marketing executives who spent years in sales. Because of their ability, they made it to the level of top management. But their careers were stunted or ruined by their unwillingness to keep going out to the market. In companies with which I have worked closely, I have encountered people who simply would not go out anymore. They stopped going, stopped being effective and eventually had to be replaced.

Most of the leaders of excellent companies have come from operations backgrounds. They have been around design, manufacturing or the selling of the product, so they are comfortable with the nuts and bolts of the business. Going out is easy for them because they are comfortable in the field. They travel more, and they spend more time with junior executives in the front line. They demonstrate the absolute need for knowing what is happening now, and with that knowledge, controlling to a substantial degree the dynamic role of the future. It is indeed possible to define the future through concrete plans that will make a significant difference in the achievements of the business. Psychiatrists say that a human being has his future within him. That is demonstrably true in business.

The most effective leaders know that they cannot delegate the crucial part of their jobs: the actual leadership function. Leadership is a quality that is difficult to define in the abstract. Real leaders—not just people who have the title—know that what they themselves do is vital to the organization, whether it is a business, an army or a nation. They know that what they do has more impact than what they say. In fact, what is said, if it is not in harmony with what is done, has little effect.

The best way to define leadership is by example. Here are a couple of classic instances of great leaders leading: General George Patton personally led the heroic rush of the Third Army in World War II to save the trapped Allied divisions in the Battle of the Bulge in 1944. He was in a lead tank, visible to the men in his army. Word of his presence at the head of the column sped down the line to the troops. Once they knew that Patton was up there, they were convinced that they were ready to do what they had to do to win, and they won.

Martin Luther King Jr. planned and organized the freedom march in Selma, Alabama, in 1962. He knew the dangers he faced. He agonized over these dangers. But when the day came, King led the march that became the vital symbol of what he was thinking and saying to his people and to the nation. He was always in the front line, always visible and vulnerable, and his supporters and his enemies knew it because they could always see him leading.

The application of this idea to business—large or small—is direct. It happens without memos or committee meetings or bulletins or newsletters. It happens. Everyone who works for the organization sees what management is about. They know that there is a willingness at the top to go out to the market to meet, to

15.
When top managers go to the front line, the entire organization benefits.

talk, to ask, to listen to what the market is saying about the company, the products, the competition.

Management then becomes a powerful, visible and dramatic symbol for the company. When this happens, it is easy to see the reaction of the senior people in the various disciplines of the organization. Some will respond quickly and begin to duplicate this style. And when they return from the market, the word will spread. Others will follow. Those who decide to work as before will find themselves less informed, less important and, if they refuse to change, gone.

The organization will change. This can happen with an organization of fifty people or five thousand. The change in the way management works provides the electric pulse that makes the business run. If half of management's time is spent away from the home office, no meeting or memo will be needed to communicate what other people in the organization must do. The change in style and purpose of the organization will be evident when the question, "Where is the boss?" is answered with, "He's out there."

But this is more than a symbolic act for the manager. There is the change that occurs within the mind and the spirit as top managers meet one-to-one with a cross-section of the market, with plant people, shippers, salespeople, wholesalers, distributors, dealers, retailers and consumers. There are questions and more questions. There is much talk about the business. There are hours of listening. There is the enormous stimulation that comes from thousands and thousands of words and sights and touches and tastes. All the senses are engaged. There is excitement. In a compact form, there is the comparable effect of a prisoner released from solitary confinement and then let out of prison altogether. This exaggeration is deliberate and symbolizes a dramatic comparison to a home-office-bound management suddenly freed to go out and see what it is like "out there."

John Doyle, head of Research and Development at Hewlett Packard, says in the book *In Search of Excellence*, "The only posture that has a chance of surviving the ravages of time is one that is unfailingly externally focused. The only way you're going to survive in the long haul is if everybody's out there scratching, looking for things to do to get the next product generation into the customer's premises."

A strong impact on the organization cannot be achieved by a token effort at market-oriented management. An occasional trip will achieve little for the manager or the organization. A trip with two or three members of the staff along will achieve less, because 75 percent of the time will be spent talking to each other rather than to people in the market. The importance of the leaders going out alone is impressed upon all the people in the organization and in the chain, from the plant to the customer.

Going to the market with an entourage is a waste of time. One sales manager I worked with always wanted to have a couple of other home-office people come along. It made the traveling more pleasant, but it was, in effect, simply carrying the home-office mentality to the field. As a group, they were not effective.

There are certain reflective symbols over and above management being out there in the market. When the trips involve tourist-class flights, modest motels, meals with salespeople where they normally eat, that style creates a special kind of closeness in sharp contrast to the aloofness that goes with first-class travel, waiting limos, deluxe hotels and four-star restaurants.

Here's another observation from a top executive who understands this:

> I started by delivering on my number-one promise: I have cleared my schedule so that about 60 percent of my time is available for listening, walking around, observing. I have even set aside all airplane travel time for "innovative dreaming,"—in fact that's where I am now. I previously used this time for in-basket clearing.

Where the management goes is also part of the message that directs the organization. The region traveled first gets the message. The amount of time with the production people, the salespeople, the service people, the distributors, the retailers, the consumers are all factors in defining where the company is going and how it will get there. If the time with certain of these people is intense and the visits frequent, then the message on what and who are important becomes clear to all. What is brought back from the market creates a direct reflection of the priorities of the business.

Tim was one of the brightest and most personable men I've worked with. He became the head of our Detroit office and quickly converted from being a ma-

jor producer into a far-from-effective "top management man." He held the firm belief that the key to his
new job was simply to "put in place good people and let
them do their jobs." He stopped participating. He
stopped his personal involvement. He became a kind of
glorified traffic cop rather than a true leader.

Top management can't delegate the future: "Where
are we going and how are we going to get there?"
There cannot be the faintest suggestion that some
special group of executives has the sole job of planning
the future for the business. The power to see the future
has to come from the information learned from the
market.

This vision takes time and miles, but it is there for
those who seek it. Consider instead the assignment of
the home-office staff to the future-planning task. Paper
flow and meetings become the order of the day. But
even more damaging is the use of consulting firms
brought in to do the job, to point to the future and then
have someone else do the job, whatever it turns out
to be.

A manufacturer of costume jewelry was profitable
but growth was slow. The president retired and was
replaced by a bright and energetic woman whose only
experience in jewelry was at the retail level. Immediately she was faced with the problem of designs for
the new line. She responded in the only way she knew.
She went back out to the market for a three-month trip
to twenty cities. In each market she met leading
buyers, designers and retailers. She asked and asked.
She encouraged their opinions. When she returned

she had completed her own "MBA in design." She was able to provide for design and production people with the direction they needed. She had seen the present and, from there, began to see the future. In the process she had a marvelous time and gained the respect of the people in the organization. By the end of three months she had a grasp of the business that would have required years had she chosen to work in the traditional way, in the home office and attending major conventions and market shows. She changed the business, built sales, increased profit and left the company far stronger than when she had arrived.

CHAPTER **12**

Listen to the People
Who Do the Work

LISTEN TO Ross Perot: "My first message is listen, listen, listen to the people who do the work."

Dana Corp. chairman Gerry Mitchell says, "In general, American management is no goddam good at talking to people and listening." Dana Corp. is a $3.5 billion producer of auto parts and industrial products. The company listens. Throughout their many plants, posters encourage people to say what they think and what they believe will help to increase Dana's productivity. The program produces a constant flow of letters, all of which a company executive answers. This is one of the ways Dana stays in touch with a workforce of more than thirty thousand. As you would expect, 60 percent of the responses are routine complaints, but the rest are positive, and more than a few turn out to be useful ideas.

A string of such questions can reveal strategic changes needed to achieve higher quality and more responsiveness in any company. You may wonder why a $20 million investment in a new computer system is not reaping the benefits promised by staff experts. The people using the reports will know. The objective of such interviews is to uncork the mutterings of smart but reluctant people down the line: "If they did it this way, they could cut out all that crap in the middle. But that's not my job, and I don't want to go down as a troublemaker."

Customers buy competitors' products for many reasons. Tests may not show exactly why. But if market share is only 15 percent, something is missing. A man at Chrysler put it this way: "Remember that despite our quality and design, each and every minute, most buyers worldwide decide that they don't want our cars. Why? What can we learn? What can we copy? What can we improve? These are key questions. Most executives carry around a big disadvantage—they cherish their products. After all, they live with them day in and day out. But that blinds them to why the customers may not like them as much as they do. Customers see the products through an entirely different set of lenses. Listening and adapting can be a great help to understand why."

When you go to the front line, you must go without fanfare or heavy advance warning. It is far better simply to appear, meet and talk about the business from the viewpoint of those in the market. These are not selling calls. These are question-asking calls, information-seeking calls, opinion-gathering calls. In the process, you will call on some of your biggest customers. With big customers there will be no need to ask much. The big customer will have a lot to tell you because he is interested in selling more of what your company has to offer. The bigger he is the more he'll have to say.

People learn to ski by asking, listening, observing and then by skiing. When the instructor does it right, the student follows the action down the hill, and the student improves. Psychologists, most notably Albert Bandura of Stanford, have studied this kind of learning. He points out that learning would be exceedingly laborious if people had to rely solely on the effects of their own actions to inform them what to do. His studies show that we learn most from those we regularly associate with. We ask, we listen, we learn.

I worked for years with textile maker Roger Milliken. He (and I) started the famous Milliken Breakfast Show for the fashion industry. It ran for a month every spring for years in New York City. Milliken was an innovator and a leader who believed in asking and listening. All news from the front line was interesting to him, especially if it came from people who were in the market. Roger attended every breakfast show for the entire month. He had as his guests each morning one or two or even three major Milliken customers. They all had breakfast and watched the show and the parade of fashions using Milliken fabrics. But for Milliken the key was listening to customers. He was finding out what they liked, what they didn't like, and what they wanted more of. For Milliken each breakfast became a visit to the market.

A bank executive recalled a listening program that one of his regions instituted. For about two weeks, all managers spent some time each day phoning customers, asking "How are we doing? How can I help? What else can we do?" Customer feedback was excellent. Bank morale improved, and lots of new business came in.

At Digital Equipment Corp., they rely on customers to find uses for minicomputers, rather than burdening the company with huge costs of developing and marketing applications on its own. DEC salesmen and engineers selling to other engineers nurture strong and lasting relationships with customers. An analyst wrote, "It's surprising how little they've caused their own growth. For years, they've been dragged along by interesting applications their customers came up with."

Patience is a virtue in working in the front lines. There will be those out there who are as isolated as headquarters-bound executives, convinced they have all the answers, and they will tell you so. But with more contact, in all parts of the country, the experience can be used to produce new ideas. Repetition will help generate the best kind of information gathering. The contacts with major participants in the marketplace must of course be balanced with contacts with small operators, who can also be a source of useful information. For example, natural soft drinks now sell hundreds of millions of cases a year. One of the first such drinks was developed by a small health food store owner on Third Avenue in New York City.

I was in his store shortly after he began to sell his all-natural soft drink. He insisted that I try a bottle. It had a strange and unpleasant aftertaste that suggested it had to be good for you to taste this bad. From this idea there followed dozens of more sophisticated and better-tasting versions of natural sodas that now claim a significant segment of soft-drink-industry sales.

William Colby, former director of the CIA, recently told a group of American businesspeople, "The trouble with the way you run your businesses is that you don't listen. Looked at one way, American business has one of the most wonderful intelligence-gathering networks in the world. Branches, divisions and subsidiaries everywhere. But the communication goes one way. You talk to them, tell them what to do. You don't listen."

Allen-Bradley, the Milwaukee electrical equipment manufacturer, had been pushed to the forefront not by its own researchers or engineers, but by its sophisticated customers.

In another high-technology company, the head of Research and Development has taken a two-month trip in each of the last ten years. He travels to user locations, carefully surveying what customers want and need more of. At times a program or policy that needs to be changed will be clearly defined during an interview and a corrective action taken at once. This can be effective when the people in the market are informed on the spot that "we'll take care of this as soon as I get to a telephone, and thank you for the thought."

Listening is the major objective, but that doesn't mean that you can't give effective advice on the spot when warranted. A suggestion here and a thought there can begin to add up to positive actions. Make it a rule to fix small things on the spot. Listening (and taking notes) lets the other people know you are serious. But the clearest indicator that you are serious is when something happens, either on the spot or soon after the contact, such as a directive wiping out a regulation that your contact convinced you was useless.

Other companies are also making this kind of curiosity a positive attribute. They listen to their customers. They also listen to competitors, front-line employees, suppliers, consultants, outside directors and just about anyone else who can reflect a view different from the one held inside. Something tells them that the world has changed and that, in the harsh light of the new reality, they aren't as beautiful as they once were. The mirror also tells them that unless they change they'll have trouble.

It is often possible to transfer effective ideas and programs from one customer to another customer (assuming they are not direct competitors). Years ago, a man named Amos Parrish used that principle to create a merchandising and marketing business serving department stores across the country. (I worked with Amos, who was an early and frequent flyer.) From

Filene's in Boston he would go to Rich's in Atlanta, to Carson Pirie Scott in Chicago, to I. Magnin in San Francisco to the Broadway in Los Angeles. This was before most of these stores were combined into chains such as Allied Stores and Federated. It was also before the development of centralized buying offices (mainly in New York).

As Parrish traveled, he was able to spread the word from one customer to another. He became the great listener, the great communicator and coordinator among a diverse group of major retailers. He gave specific advice such as where to locate perfumes or ladies' shoes and how big a department should be and next to what other departments and why. He knew from very successful retailers what worked best. And he had the advantage of being able to judge this from his enormous variety of sources all across the country.

Dr. Melvin Konner described the third year of medical school in a 1987 New York *Times* article in a way that relates to the work of management in the marketplace. He describes what the medical students see through "the marvelous prism of participant observation. The student is exposed to surgery, neurology, psychiatry, pediatrics, obstetrics, internal medicine, etc." He describes those moments of learning when "the crunch of clinical insight joins practical aspects of doing and then to the confirmation of the theory involved." In a different world, management should become involved with the marketplace as participant observers.

I have worked with a dozen leaders who work in

constant contact with their markets. They are as different in style as their names: Stevens, Smith, Twitchell, Friedrick, Hegi, Weinberg, Lindsey, Milliken, Lane, Thomas. Each of them works the market and each makes sure that he follows up by analyzing and using what he gathers and responding in some way to every useful contact.

Few use the same method, but they all produce a record of what they see, hear and conclude. And they all follow up these information-gathering contacts with analysis, with procedure and policy changes where warranted and with reports back to the field to let the people out there know how important these contacts were.

Each of these executives approaches follow-up in ways he himself has developed and refined over time. But each considers his or her follow-up as a vital part of management's work in the front line. They report that the process produces an accumulation of impressions and ideas to be stored away in the subconscious for later use. That is a vital part of this management attitude.

This process should include prompt recognition of your sources in the market. Send them letters that remind them of what they told you and why it was useful. That will make it mean more to them. It will show them how what they said fitted into a larger context. If possible, tell them what will be done as a result of their information. This type of follow-up has the added advantage of increasing the executive's visibility in the market. It gets the people in the market to

16. *Sort out what is important and useful for other people in the organization.*

participate in the business in a constructive, cumulative way. A note of recognition and appreciation is a clear expression to the people in the marketplace that the time spent has been productive because what they reported was valid and important to the success of the company.

CHAPTER *13*

It Is Easier To See the Future From the Marketplace

CONSIDER HOW long it took Detroit to see the urgent need for better quality in its products. Yet that need was evident in the marketplace at least fifteen years ago, evident to those who went out to see firsthand what was going on.

Consider the plight of Del Monte, long the dominant packer of canned fruits and vegetables, and long dominated by production-oriented people (some would say farmers). The market was changing, and the signs of that change were all there in the marketplace. And yet Del Monte played a pat hand year after year, losing market share and shelf space until it lost its dominant position. Sales declined year after year, net income declined and finally the sales power in this truly great brand name lost much of its strength with retailers and consumers.

Work in the marketplace, on the front lines, can be exhausting. But I believe that asking and talking and listening can produce what you must have, a deeper understanding of what is needed to strengthen the business and make it grow. One trip can trigger the thought, the plan that can make a difference in the direction of the business. There is always the potential for seeing something new and different.

I have seen too many companies in which management has played the home-office-management game until the situation became tragic for everybody. Going out into the marketplace consistently can direct the business with sensitivity to the need for change and to the forms that this change must take.

Justice Benjamin Cardozo defined seeing the future as an act of practical problem solving. He said in a lecture at his alma mater, Columbia University in 1927:

> Start with successive stages of preparation and then more preparation. And when the subject is known, truly known, truly understood, then the matter can be put away for a time to incubate, to cook, to bubble and boil so that one day the idea, the answer being sought, will come to light, come to light ever so bright as though by magic.

Let me assure you that it is not magical at all. It is, instead, the product of effort and of gathering information from a variety of sources, all illuminating, all stimulating, all working in the mind of the singular man.

Solutions do not come from the blue; they come from hard work, and commitment to the task. It is important to recognize the tremendous potential that comes from storing in the mind the myriad bits of information from the marketplace. Then the power of the subconscious mind will come to the fore and produce solutions that are new and different and, most important of all, practical. It is this creative process that can provide the vital look into the future. That is the process that explains the countless instances in which leading business executives worry at a problem, then set it aside only to find the answer—seemingly arriving from nowhere—staring back at them from the mirror in the morning.

Although intuition is not discussed much in business, it has always played a vital role. The most successful managers use intuition regularly in planning and decision making. Professor Henry Mintzberg of McGill University concludes from extensive study that the best managers are intuitive thinkers who rely constantly on hunches to cope with problems too complex for rational analysis.

John Dewey stated it this way:

Unconsciousness gives spontaneity and freshness; consciousness, command and control. The conscious can be likened to the part of a recipe which accumulates and prepares the various ingredients of, say, a well-seasoned casserole. The unconscious is the closed oven in which the casserole, while cooking slowly, draws on the heat of the oven to bring out the unrealized succulence of the herbs. In fulfilling an objective, the conscious gathers and weighs the facts, the unconscious

113

simmers them and produces order out of their chaos. Then the conscious mind takes over again and uses its power to produce new plans, new ideas.

The job of forecasting becomes even more difficult as an increasing number of businesses, such as mine, enter international markets. Planners then have to consider such factors as currency fluctuations. Foreign-exchange transactions now total $80 trillion a year, only $4 trillion of which is required to finance trade in goods and services. The rest is speculation. The prices of the major currencies, which used to fluctuate no more than 1 percent or so over years, now swing 5 to 10 percent a week, and up to 50 percent a year. The prices of energy, agricultural products and metals are often just as volatile.

Using a home-office staff to plan the future is dubious for good reason. The process becomes too theoretical because it is based on factors that are difficult to track. Plans created by headquarters staffers, using computer analyses, often don't consider the unimaginable, and what you least expect is what often happens. Harvard's renowned marketing professor Theodore Levitt believes that modelers build intricate decision trees whose pretension to utility is exceeded only by the awe in which high-level line managers hold the technocrats who construct them. Effective planning depends on executive experience in the field.

Fletcher Byrom of Koppers Corp. offered this comment: "As a regimen, as a discipline for a group of people, planning is very valuable. My position is, go ahead and plan, but once you've done your planning, put it on the shelf. Don't be bound by it. Don't use it as a major input to the decision-making process. Use it mainly to recognize change as it takes place."

In a similar comment, Business Week has reported: "Significantly, neither Johnson & Johnson, nor TRW, nor 3M—regarded as forward thinking—has anyone on board called a corporate planner."

Formal planning as a staff function is not the way to see what the future may hold. Operating managers must do the job themselves; they cannot delegate it, because it requires intimate knowledge of what is going on at the front line. Just as important, looking to the future in a productive way must include the kind of experimentation that involves recognition of the prospect of failure. Failure is not to be contemplated at headquarters; only well-oiled perfection is allowed.

In *Thriving on Chaos* by Tom Peters, Soichiro Honda, founder of Honda Motor says, "Many people dream of success. To me success can only be achieved through repeated failure and introspection. In fact, success represents the 1 percent of your work that results only from the 99 percent that is called failure." Also in the same book, Gordon Forward, president of Chaparral Steel, reports, "You've got to have an atmosphere where people can make mistakes. If we're not making mistakes, we're not going anywhere. The scientific method is designed for mistakes."

Emerson Electric's Charles Knight believes that a manager needs the ability to fail and that it is difficult to innovate unless one is willing to accept mistakes.

Johnson & Johnson's James Burke said in a New York *Times* article that one of J&J's tenets is "you've got to be willing to fail." He adds that General Johnson, J&J's founder, said to him, "If I wasn't making mistakes, I wasn't making decisions."

"For God's sake, go down to reception and get rid of a lunatic who is down there. He says he's got a machine for seeing by wireless. Watch him; he may have a razor on him," said the editor of the Daily Express of London, refusing to see John Baird, the inventor of television, in 1925.

When philosopher William James was asked what comes before a conclusion, he replied, "When the conclusion is there, we have already forgotten most of the steps preceding its attainment."

In my experience, after prolonged exposure to a problem, the mind ceases to work on it effectively. It seems to be in a rut; the wheels go around in the head, but they do not turn out anything fresh. This condition is a warning to turn your conscious attention and reflection to something else. Then, after the mind has stopped focusing consciously on the problem, a period of incubation sets in. Material rearranges itself; facts and principles fall into place; what was confused becomes clear often to such an extent that the problem is essentially solved.

But be warned that the subconscious will not produce anything of value unless it has been fed with a lot of hard work studying the problem and gathering first-hand information.

Jacques Hadamard, the French mathematician, has

17. *With intense personal knowledge of the market, a long-term strategy will inevitably emerge.*

observed: "I had worked for months on a particular problem. Then, on being very abruptly awakened by a loud noise, a solution long searched for appeared to me at once without the slightest instant of reflection on my part, the fact was remarkable enough to have struck me unforgettably, and in a quite different direction from any of those which I had previously tried to follow."

Yet, again and again, companies and leaders go to work on the wrong problems. The key factor is defined by Georges Bernanos, the French novelist and theologian, who stated, "The worst and most corrupting lies are about problems inaccurately defined and incorrectly understood but, it happens all the time."

American Motors attempted again and again to design and produce automobiles that would be more competitive in the marketplace. In fact, the problem was simply that the company was too small to compete in the industry against GM and Ford. It lacked the financial and human resources and the dealers to be competitive in the industry.

Schlitz Brewing's concern with trying to combat the problem of growth of the new lighter beers led the company to conclude that its problem was its brewing formulas. So it changed them. New formulas were developed and new beers were produced, but the old Schlitz drinkers deserted the brand. Schlitz should not have played around with a proven formula and a dedicated market segment. They worked on the wrong problem and came up with a wrong solution.

Military surgeons working during wars long ago recognized that not all of the problems of the wounded can be solved. So they adopted the process known as triage and classified wounded as they came in into three categories: (1) the superficially wounded, (2) the seriously wounded who have a chance, (3) the hopeless. Then they devote all of their energies and time to those who have a chance.

In business, the same situation often develops. There are problems beyond solution. Not recognizing that and persisting in trying to solve the unsolvable produces enormous waste of effort and money.

It is of course absolutely essential to define a problem precisely to determine if it is real and solvable. There's no formula for achieving this. Anyone who would suggest there is probably is a business-school professor, a consultant or a fool—or maybe all three.

Too much history and too much time at the home office can make problem-definition difficult. Business problems cannot be identified accurately without experience of the marketplace. Change in the market cannot be understood from reading reports or attending home-office meetings. Awareness of the rate of change and a sense of the future come to managers who work consistently in the market and confront the differences between problems that can be solved and those that can't.

Five-year plans that have to be revised every year are the rule in most companies, so they become a kind of bad joke. Historical trends projected as straight lines—

or by any other formula—don't work. So plans are developed, then revised every year. Changes in most industries and companies come with greater speed and scope and in more diverse directions than ever before. It is true of course that in earlier times, the business world seemed more stable and therefore more predictable. But, clearly, not anymore. There are ways to look into the future and to plan successfully, but they differ from those of the past.

In the past, some trend lines could be relied on for casting sales growth, margins, operating expenses and operating profits. The computers seemed to work to produce fairly reliable views of what the company's world would look like five years into the future. As long as everything in the economy was booming, as it did for decades after World War II, the level of accuracy was at least acceptable. Corporate boards liked this kind of planning with its hard numbers, ratios and trend lines. There was comfort and even joy in such plans.

Economic models were developed in a lot of places, notably at such business schools as Wharton and MIT. These models were based on dozens of assumptions about the shape of the future. A new school of economic theory seems to be emerging that concludes that the factors that influence the future are so numerous and unpredictable that long-range projections are all but impossible.

What is wrong is not the idea of trying to plan five years ahead. The error is trying to create a five-year plan on the basis of performance over prior years. You can't ignore the past, of course. But you can no longer expect it to be a definitive guide to anything as far in the future as five years.

The future has to be a primary concern to top management. Speculation about where your business will be in two or five years is useful. We cannot ignore history, but we cannot depend upon history and past experience alone in planning. The traditional five-year plan based on recent history and mathematical projections is simply not adequate. In a dynamically changing business environment, we need precise personal knowledge of the present to plan the future.

The more you know about your business today, the better you can determine what it will be like in the future. But the future will not be like the past. We have to use past experience every day in every contact and every decision. The history of your business and your industry is useful, but too much reliance on history and past experience will inevitably produce distortions.

For decades, the American automobile industry controlled the world. Clearly that is no longer the case. The industry is now fighting to hang on to its dwindling market share, because it failed to respond to such basic considerations as gas mileage performance, quality-control standards, the appeal of the small car and sophisticated styling. Why? Because the people at the top saw the world through their record of the past.

I remember the sheer arrogance of a top executive at GM's Buick who said, "Hell, I'm not worried about what Mercury or Chrysler are doing; my competition is Olds and Pontiac. They're the really tough ones to pound against." Of course he didn't see the enormous threat of the Germans and then the Japanese. Why not? Because he never left his office and never even drove through the neighborhoods where the products of his foreign competitors were beginning to show up as early as the 1960s. His interest was in satisfying his superiors at headquarters, not in keeping in touch with the realities of his market.

Another part of the problem rests in the need for constant short-term income projections. Reginald Jones, after retiring as CEO of General Electric, said that "too many managers feel under pressure to satisfy the income performance of the financial community and the owners of the enterprise, the stockholders. In the United States, if a firm has a bad quarter, it's headlines. Real trouble ensues. The stock price falls out of bed. That's far different from Japan and Germany." In the United States, Wall Street raises the capital and demands immediate results. Among the strengths of Japanese and German industry are that as much as 80 percent of their permanent capital is provided by banks, with companies grouped around major banks like satellites.

"Some executives in America," says a vice-president of LTV, "try to deal with long-range problems in the short run. They want to demonstrate that they'll meet this year's targets this year. What gets lost is the strategy that will move the company over twenty-five to thirty years."

The whole idea of such emphasis on quarter-by-quarter results is wrong. And the constant comparison to the past is an inherent part of the problem. Projecting for one year is not easy. Two years is difficult. Five years is impossible. Yet the five-year plans keep rolling out, waiting, of course, for the annual fix. The future has to be planned on a sounder basis than solely on the trend lines of the past.

CHAPTER **14**

A New Approach To Financial Planning

THIS PLAN has unique safety features that will help to reduce the surprises from big variations that hurt cash flow and net income. It brings a practical approach to this important process. The basic premise of this book is to urge management to use personal exposure to the marketplace as their guide to the business. Financial planning should involve a similarly hard-edged method. The days of getting away with fanciful five-year plans are long over. That is too dangerous a way to operate. These days you have to use a tougher, smarter method for your financial planning. Before I get to this approach, let's look at how most financial plans are developed.

The five-year financial plan is still widely used despite the fact that it works only for those companies that have a surging pattern of sales growth, up 15 percent to 20 percent or more each year. The five-year plan works in those instances because the sales growth often compensates for unexpected changes in expenses, materials costs, economic changes, new product failures and all the other things that cannot be planned accurately.

Typically, however, five-year plans have to be revised every year, because the actual results rarely match the plan. That is, of course, because the first year almost invariably is easier to forecast than those that follow. The inherent difficulties of seeing into the future increase the further you look. Who knows what the new product will do; what the competition will come up with; how the economy, commodity costs, industry pricing will behave; or what the effects will be on gross margins. The answer, of course, is no one. Luck—good and bad—affects every aspect of life including five-year plans.

The problem of projecting sales and controlling expenses is part of the routine of doing business for most companies. The only ones that escape are those lucky enough to enjoy endless growth periods. Few of us who run businesses have such good fortune.

I've worked with five-year plans affected by all these unpredictable forces. So what is the answer? One-year plans are too limited. You have to think further ahead if you are running anything bigger than a corner grocery store.

Some years ago I ran into an idea that became popular for a time. It was created by a financial man who called his method the Rolling 12 Plan.

Every quarter actual sales are compared to budget. Then sales for the next twelve months are projected against the quarter just completed. And, of course, expenses and profit for the twelve months are also adjusted. That seems right at first glance because it always tells you exactly where the business is going for any twelve-month period as a projection of the most current quarterly results.

The problem with a Rolling 12 Plan is that it keeps everyone in the organization in a constant state of flux. Sales objectives are constantly changing. When sales are off, the business goes into a binge of cost cutting. The Rolling 12 Plan removes set goals from sales and set objectives from expenses and profit. Some financial people love the Rolling 12. It always keeps them in what appears to be a secure position. The trouble is that it keeps everyone else in the business in an ambivalent state. The business gets softer and softer. I've seen it happen. The five-year plan is too long. The one-year plan is too short. The Rolling 12 Plan produces chaos.

The two-year financial plan works because it looks into the future just far enough but not too far. I have used it in the past seven years in my own business, The Monarch Company. I developed it after years of using the traditional method of financial planning. Then expenses were planned to support the sales projections. Again and again, the sales projections fell short, typically because of the natural optimism of salespeople. (The better they were, the more likely they were to be excessively optimistic.) When sales fall short, there

18. *Five-year plans get changed every year, so don't make them.*

follows the arduous process of cutting back expenses to try to hold onto the planned operating income. But the cutback was invariably too late, typically about six months too late. So there goes a piece of the planned income.

This plan provides a control on expenses that can work to the satisfaction of both sales and financial executives. It works because it brings to financial planning a sense of reality. The two-year plan must start from scratch. The first year does use projected sales and projected expenses. Both factors start in a proper relationship. Here's how it works:

1. Sales are projected for two twelve-month periods. There's some reach. But sales managers can be comfortable and tough about sales objectives in Year One and also in Year Two. The period is short enough to take into account such variables as new products, product line changes, important price changes, commodity costs, economic conditions, new incentive plans, competitive actions and variations in support programs such as advertising.

   The Year One sales projection is as detailed as possible, given the experience of the two or three years just completed. Year Two should be just as detailed. The best two-year plans make distinctions only in the projections for each twelve-month period. The same projection effort is put into the full twenty-four-month period. The two years give the sales projection a chance to come close.

A two-year projection gets serious. It is short enough to be accurate and, with appropriate pressure on the sales operation, to perform to the numbers. A five-year projection is "game playing."
2. Raw material costs are as important to sales projections as price increases. Both can significantly affect gross profit margins and have an impact on the sales projections in the two years.
3. Operating expenses in the two-year financial plan are handled differently. The premise is that sales growth in a single year should not automatically produce commensurate operating expense growth in the second year. Operating expense changes should lag one year behind. *Operating expenses should not automatically increase with an increase in sales in the second year of the two-year plan.*

Cutting back expenses is tough work when sales are off. You can't cut expenses after two months in a year when sales have started off below projections, because that is usually too early. So you wait for the fifth or sixth month of actual sales to see what cutting of selling expenses is needed. But that is usually too late. The longer you wait, the more accurate the cuts, but the less effective they are in the remaining months of the year. Cut too early, and that can harm the sales effort. Cut after six months or more, and the saving isn't enough to protect projected profits for the year.

The two-year process is continuous. Every two years a new two-year plan is prepared. Assume there is

19. *The key to the two-year plan is how expenses are projected in the second year.*

steady sales growth in both years of the plan. *For the second year, expenses are not allowed to increase, so profit can increase.* And there is another two-year plan ahead. If sales don't increase in Year Two, the company profit is protected. And so it goes with successive two-year financial plans.

The premise that sales growth warrants expense growth is valid only if that sales growth occurs in Year One and is not based on projections for Year Two.

Of course there has to be some flexibility. There always are some operating expenses that increase almost automatically and are beyond the control of the financial plan. Salary increases have to be based on the cost of living. But increases in sales personnel have to be level in Year Two. The same for advertising and promotion.

Does this punish sales? Maybe. But when sales projections are not met and expenses have been increased based on a bigger projection, does this punish the company and diminish net income? Of course. The premise is simple: a company or division whose sales growth is based on projections should only earn the right to spend more money after producing more sales, not before.

20. *The two-year financial plan works for financial planning and works for expense control.*

CHAPTER *15*

Planning Major Changes

IT IS important to separate the planning of major changes in your business from the push-and-pull of annual performance, because it requires quite a different kind of thinking. The most effective way to do this, I have found, is simply to create another kind of plan, something I call the major change plan. Don't think about numbers and projections at the start of this process. Instead try to take a different approach to your business, and ask yourself these kinds of questions: Is there a real growth opportunity? If so, where should it come from? What does the market say? What are competitors doing? Where are the problems in the business? Where are the problems in the industry? And so on.

The answers will, of course, come from the market and from all the sources in the market that can help define real problems and opportunities. They will not come from reading, from committee reports, from consultants, from independent research projects. Major-change plans do not develop quickly. The ideas come from an accumulation of ideas gathered over time in the marketplace. That is where you find the full range of practical possibilities for your business and your industry covering new products, plant openings and closings, production efficiency, expansion into new markets, acquisitions, dispositions and all the rest.

Major-change planning is not simple. It requires a life of its own, it must be separate from the work that produces the two-year financial plan. The major change plan is a capital-use process. There was a time when such capital was ideally generated out of accumulated excess cash flow from the operations of the business. Nothing wrong with this if it does the job. Other sources, of course, are stock issues, borrowing, asset sales, and so on. Determining which of these methods, separately or in combination, should be used by a business is what we are dealing with in the major-change plan. Separating the two-year financial plan from the major-change plan in terms of capital sources and accumulation improves both functions.

The two-year financial plan should run with its own resources and with its own capital generation. Consider the case of a large advertising agency group that tried to support its plans for growth by pulling capital from its operating components. This required the operating companies to cut back on staff and client service to produce the capital that the parent needed for its growth plan. The resulting personnel cuts reduced performance quality and eventually lost clients.

The difficulties of the U.S. automobile industry, with its vast capital investments, have come mostly from its inability to distinguish in its planning between short- and long-term needs and opportunities. Lewis Young, while editor of *Business Week*, wrote in that magazine "The top managements (all of them) were blinded by the short-term numbers, the profits of large cars, the advantage of big numbers of production models, and penny-pinching on the fits and finishes." In other words, they had not figured out how to make major-change plans.

Major-change planning, long-term planning, strategic planning, whatever you call it, barely exists in such companies because they are driven by yearly performance. Once the numbers are in the bag for the year, the pressure to think about the future is off until next year's numbers game begins.

The business schools must take much of the blame for this short-term orientation. For years they have been supplying the world with MBAs who, because of their training, especially in finance, believe that they can manage any business by reading the numbers. We are coming to recognize that numbers orientation without knowledge of the products in the market is worse than useless; it is dangerous. It tends to shut off long-range planning. It tends to ignore the in-depth knowledge that has to be the source for work and major changes in a business.

At Sony Corp. of America, Michael Schulhof, in a Chicago *Tribune* article, talks about the impact of American business schools and their products, the

MBAs. "The short-term and frequently shortsighted positions win out with disturbing regularity because American business is top-heavy with the ever-expanding numbers of business-school graduates who are trained advocates of the short-term profit." Schulhof adds, "It is not entirely coincidence that the same years that have seen industry increasingly, almost exclusively, run by financially oriented business-school graduates have also seen the worst productivity performance since the Depression."

Kenneth Mason, former CEO of Quaker Oats Co., has added his thinking about short-term plans without the important work of major-change plans to form the basis for a company's growth over the long term. He believes that the top executives of an incredibly large number of America's best-known corporations spend hundreds of man-hours a year, year after year, making sure not only that this year's annual earnings increase is consistent with last year's, but that this year's third quarter doesn't fall below last year's third quarter, or that this year's third quarter isn't so good that next year's third quarter won't be able to top it, or that this year's third quarter won't embarrass this year's fourth quarter, and so on and on.

A growing number of top management people are becoming aware of these problems; at least they are talking about them. A recent poll showed that one in three believed that most of the managers in charge don't know enough about their markets, about innovation and about technology. Technology and innovation have no numbers; they are future-oriented.

David Vogel of the business school at the University of California at Berkeley has noted that the nations with the most developed systems of professional management education, the United States and Great Britain, are performing poorly, when two nations that provide almost no professional management training, Germany and Japan, have been the outstanding successes of the postwar period.

But there are signs of a shift from the short-term outlook to long-term, major-change planning. One top executive has said, "Boards of directors have to understand that they must shelter management from the pressure of short-term results in the interest of the corporation itself and in the interest of the nation. The board has got to concern itself with the long-range future of the business and not be that upset by a bad quarter or a bad year so long as productive and cost-effective spending is going on for the long range."

Business Week also comments that "companies can change the signals that push their own people away from long-term vision into shorter myopia. They can reaffirm the need for basic research, for taking risks, for planning for the long haul. And they can create a climate in which educated risk-takers feel that their jobs are secure and that their willingness to take risks is appreciated."

Schlumberger, the French company that invented the electronic data processes that help locate oil and define wells, has for some time been planning major changes in the face of competition and the inevitable end of oil exploration. The company is expanding into broader areas of data collection and processing before the oil-drilling business recedes, even though this expansion will not produce commensurate profits immediately.

Sears, Roebuck & Co. is another example of a company that has tried to confront the need to go beyond its original businesses, but maybe too late. In late 1981 the giant retailer embarked on a daring new strategy: Stay in retailing but also use its retail locations to offer its customers financial services. Sears bought big companies in securities and real estate brokering. The company's strategic moves have not yet worked as well as its executives had hoped. They simply may not have moved quickly enough—not preparing their existing retail customers to use their stores to buy stocks and bonds, real estate and mortgages. What is more, the company seems to have been moved by its retailing competitors, rather than moving ahead of them, into new pricing policies for its stores. Nevertheless, Sears continues to see itself as a retailer, but with much broader lines of services.

Major-change plans must be developed separate from the main operating plan for the business, because when you base major changes on a separate plan, your thinking will become tougher. You will confront the prospect of financial losses from the failure of these planned major changes. You will, to be sure, often derive at least some of your major-change capital from the excess cash flow generated by your shorter term plans. But by separating the resources you propose to use from those of the normal operation of the business,

21. *Never assign long-term planning to a staff group.*

you reduce the chance of burying long-term expenses in results of the operating units. This way, major-change plans are out in the open. They work or they don't. There is no place for them to hide.

Digital Equipment Corp. was started from scratch by Kenneth Olsen. It now employs more than one hundred thousand people. Here's what Olsen has to say about keeping the dollar of profit on the mind:

"With success and with growth it is easy to let the planning and gross profit margin control be done by staff. But the leader without gross profit dollars and the P&L in his head and in his heart every minute of every day has no power. He loses control of the business. He loses the necessary emphasis on what the business is all about. This happens so easily that the loss is not noticed. The home-office financial staff takes control, and, in some cases they can begin to believe that the numbers are 'their numbers,' without recognizing the separation between the actions of the company and the job of totaling up the final results in dollars."

With the growth of staff people, central planning emerged, and the big part of such planning came from the financial staff. The ritual of the quarterly review, with all the figures always up, demonstrates the separation of profit control from the daily consciousness of management. The quarterly review must never be the first time that top managers see results. They should already know the results because they have every gross profit margin and end result in mind just about every minute of every day.

CHAPTER 16

All the Dollars Are Real

A DOLLAR is never an abstraction to the entrepreneur who mortgages his house, uses all his savings and borrows on his personal guarantee to create a business. He thinks hard about every dollar spent. This is a habit, a fundamental attitude that, in too many companies, has been lost.

The home-office environment produces a far different attitude. There is an exaggerated sense of influence and importance that makes the spending of money almost casual at times. Travel is first-class. Expensive meals are routine. Limousines are a measure of accomplishment. Country club memberships are an accepted part of the scene. All this produces a mentality that can be dangerous when such matters as new products, programs and plants are under consideration. Risk factors are often not considered accurately in such an environment. The reality is that style and political relationships can overwhelm sound judgment. Serious concerns about expenditures somehow become secondary.

Sometimes the dollar being spent is not real, not "mine," but somebody else's dollar. Bankers should be the exception. They only deal in money. It's all they think about, but unfortunately some do not think hard enough about the dollars they lend. L. Carter Bacot, chairman of the Bank of New York, has dramatically changed this old institution in just a few years. He has approached the job as though he owned the bank and the dollars being spent were all his own. The bank's operating expenses were reduced in just three years from 61.4 percent, the average of the other large banks in New York, to 58.2 percent, a drop of 3.2 percent. And that all went to the bottom line. The profits of the bank surged from a 0.60 percent return on assets to 0.82 percent, an increase of more than 33 percent. Bacot works directly with every department and every branch of the bank. He is rarely in his own office. He thinks hard about the dollars being spent and lent as though they were his own.

The credit card is the simplest expression of the abstract dollar. Its use and the expense account in general are common contributors to what has become a lack of respect for a company's dollars. Limousines, first-class airfare, deluxe hotels, should not be necessities for anybody in the company. Think about it: Is the thinking and the work done in first class any better than that done in tourist? The ultimate expression of this conversion of real money into abstraction is the corporate jet with pilots standing by around the clock.

This may appear to be petty harping about a few dollars. True, those specific dollars do not mean much in most operating statements. But the message that is communicated to the organization by this type of spending of "other people's money" can mean a lot. It is not a matter of saving a dollar here or there. Instead, it is the focusing of the entire organization's attitude on the dollar and on whether it would be spent if it were "my dollar."

I recently worked with a large European company that had a significant investment in a U.S. company that was losing money. The French executive assigned to this problem traveled only first-class and stayed only in such luxurious hotels as the Plaza in New York and the Stanford Court in San Francisco. He often held budget-control meetings with local managers of the company in his hotel suite. He saw no contradiction between the serious financial problems they were working on and his style of traveling.

Staff executives usually can't be relied upon to think in terms of the money they allocate being "my dollar." The distance of the staff from the front line, from the marketplace, creates the distance from the realities of money. The monthly or quarterly review of financial results becomes just another report. Staff people don't feel the pain of misspent dollars. Their mindset is that the money belongs to faceless shareholders, who don't have much, if anything, to say.

But attitudes of staff people can be directly influenced by the mind-set of management. If top executives really act as though all the dollars being spent are

22. *Do you think smarter in first class than in tourist?*

"my dollar," then the odds are that every dollar spent will be weighed carefully. This requires discipline on every project. The need is to instill this "my dollar" attitude in the entire organization. It comes from the top and flows down. It will not develop at the bottom and work its way up.

In England a few years ago, a board of directors meeting spent more than two hours discussing a plan to build a new bicycle shed for workers that would have cost seven thousand dollars. At the same meeting, construction of a new North Country plant was approved in just 20 minutes. The cost was projected at $20.2 million. But the bicycle shed was closer to home.

When the organization truly thinks and plans and spends only "my dollar," a wondrous change takes place. When it is "my dollar," the evaluation gets tough for:

- The home-office staff
- The look of the offices
- Every new product
- Every test market
- The size of the price increase
- Every gross profit margin
- First class or economy
- Hotel or motel
- Where the big meeting will be held
- The exploratory trip abroad
- The existing plant
- The obsolete plant

23. *Constant awareness of gross profit margins, cost control and cash flow does wonders for management.*

Some years ago, in his "Managing for Results," Peter Drucker made the point that gross profit margins by product and product line were of vital importance to a company, to its performance, to its direction and to its profit performance. Gross profit must be determined at the inception of a new product idea. Thinking about P&L is important, but before everything comes gross profit margin. That is obvious today, and yet plans and products are still developed without early consideration of gross profit margin by everyone involved in planning and development—particularly top management, the decision-makers.

Product development and marketing people must have full understanding of the gross profit function in all their planning. But they often do not, and top management often has to stop a project because there is not enough gross margin potential. Only about one in twenty new products makes it all the way to a profitable lifespan. And more than half of new product failures are directly related to inadequate gross profit margins.

When awareness of gross profit and P&L penetrates the entire organization from top to bottom, every expense no matter how small becomes important, not just for the dollars involved, but for the symbolic effect. A lavish business lifestyle for top management can affect everyone. So there should be no room for the grand style. Perceptive leaders know this and give up the small pleasures of big spending on themselves. That is a matter of integrity in the business. The size of the office was once a symbol of achievement and power, the summit achieved, so to speak. But now policy on office size is changing. "All the same size" has become an expression of the new style of smart executives. The office doesn't have to speak for the executive. He needs some space, a desk and little more. Some top managers have given up the private office completely. Instead they do their work, when at the home office, in the offices of other people. What will major customers think when the big, corner office is no more? If it becomes an issue, it doesn't take much to explain, and the explanation invariably produces positive reactions. True leadership comes from the character of the leader, not from the size of his office.

Again, Kenneth Olsen, in a New York *Times* interview in 1988 advises, "I tell them, when they pray at night, to pray about their P&L statement. If your P&L statement is not so simple you can't remember every line, or if it's not yours and not in your spirit and in your stomach, you do not know what you want and you don't know what your plans are."

As Robert Townsend, says in his book *Up the Organization*, "No accounting system is very good and all of them are infinitely variable. The easiest way to do a snow job on management is to make the financial report so detailed and so complex that it becomes difficult to separate the major factors from the minor."

Citicorp's Larry Small believes that there isn't a company in the world that is really a good one that isn't excellent at cost control. IBM can tell you down to hundredths of a cent what each piece of wire costs in every single piece of machinery they make. A call on the chairman of McDonald's inevitably ends up in a discussion about some infinite detail of managing costs in the hamburger business, such as the number of washes you can get before a plastic tray loses its luster and has to be discarded. When our people visited Milliken and Co., perhaps the largest private textile company in the world, they were always surprised to see that whether it was the personnel specialist or financial controller taking them on the factory floor, they all knew the operation inside out and could talk about nothing other than how to increase productivity and profit.

In a similar but far more simple way, old-time coal miners had a need for constant awareness when they went to work in the depths of the mines. It was dark and dangerous down there. So they carried singing canaries into the mines. When the singing stopped and the bird died, the miners knew that the air was deadly with gases and that their lives were in danger.

Management has a similar need for sensitivity. Every subject, every project, must be measured as a direct reflection of the gross profit margins, cost controls and cash flow.

24. *Business leaders should carry a canary in their heads.*

CHAPTER 17

The Most Effective Product Development Starts in the Marketplace

LEON LEONWOOD Bean, the renowned mail-order wizard known as L.L. Bean, started his business in 1912 with a fundamental product development approach that is still being used by the company today. The products had to be "tried, true and tested by people who hunt and fish." At L.L. Bean there has been no change in this philosophy over the years. In the Carrabassett Valley of Maine, the contacts with sportsmen and the flow of new products continue. The product development at Bean starts in the woods and streams and then moves to the design rooms for refinement and improvement.

In a more sophisticated product development arena, such as Silicon Valley, this type of approach often meets with disdain. Here is a typical attitude: "What can I possibly learn out there talking to people who

Frank A. Armstrong

can't begin to understand what I'm about, much less understand what I say. They are not smart enough to help me in my work." In *Research Policy* magazine, Modesto Madque and Jo Zirger report a study in the electronics industry on 150 products. Half worked. Half failed. They report that "unsuccessful products were often technological marvels that received technical excellence awards and were written up in prestigious journals." Too much exotic technology at far too high a price is the story of virtually every one of the product failures. In contrast, the successful products almost always have been exposed to customer evaluations and recommendations.

A growing requirement in many product development operations is to send people out into the marketplace. This does not suggest that complex technical developments will come directly from people in the front line. But the exposure can stimulate the technical mind in ways that no amount of laboratory work can.

Sony developed the world-famed and much-copied Walkman portable cassette player simply by observing youngsters on roller skates listening to and moving to the rhythm of rock music played on small portable radios. "Why not give them the exact type of music they want when they want it?"

The automobile industry has generally given management people the opportunity to drive all its cars. The cars are always new, checked out carefully, tuned and cleaned. But not enough time is spent driving cars that have been out on the road driven by a hard-driving salesman who put fifty thousand miles on the car in six

154

months. Such cars would "talk" to management in important ways. What is more, auto executives never endure the ordeal of trying to buy a car or have it serviced by a dealer. These are among the most painful events American car owners have to confront. In fact, many people lie and claim they paid less for their cars than they actually did because they are ashamed to admit that they were railroaded by the salesman.

Buying their own and driving used cars would be even more useful than simply receiving new and well-serviced company products every three months. And they should drive a different competitor's model every week: American, Japanese, German, Swedish, Korean. Consider what this policy could have produced back in the early 1970s when foreign competition and then the first gasoline shortage hit the industry.

Most packaged-goods companies use extensive test marketing on new products. The problem is that this work is most often done by junior staff marketing people. What they see and hear and learn from this research is much different from what would happen if the people in product development were out there working and talking and listening to the marketplace. The product-development people would bring a perspective to the work that is vital. They would see and listen and be stimulated by the exposure in a unique way. The old methodology is cumbersome, time-consuming and not sensitive enough. When the best minds, the most experienced product developers, go out, they can create the breakthroughs that are needed.

25. *The Japanese start product development work by going to the market first.*

The economist Christopher Freeman analyzed thirty-nine innovations in the chemical industry and thirty-three in scientific instruments. The number-one factor for success was the same in both industries. He determined that successful firms understand user needs better. He also found that the number-two factor was reliability for both categories. Successful innovations, he concluded, have fewer problems.

In the totally different field of high-quality furniture, a major manufacturer has taken a similar approach. The company wanted to do more than just use the designs developed by its own staff people. It gathered a group of the top designers and decorators in Baltimore to obtain their ideas about the industry's products, not just their own line. The first meeting worked well, and as a result the program was carried to other cities, where the top designers were brought together for their advice. The result for the company was major changes in product design, in production methods, in prices and a significant increase in sales and profit.

In the automobile industry, Ford has led the way as the first of the Big Three to recognize the power of the Japanese in the market. They knew that their main competitor was Toyota and created the successful Taurus and Sable in response. Meanwhile, GM was still in the old mode. They recognized neither the Japanese nor Ford nor Chrysler.

Japanese management expert Henichi Ohmae is quoted in Tom Peters's *Thriving on Chaos*, "The most successful Japanese consumer electronics companies send their product-design engineers around the world

26.   *From the start, product cost and product profit must be a vital part of new product development.*

for about six months each year to study the latest
customer needs and survey the competitive scene.
They visit customers and dealers. They attend trade
shows. They hold regional product conferences with
dealers and salesmen." And, as we know, they have a
high ratio of success in product innovations.

When Honda launched the upscale Acura, it selected BMW as its leading competitor. The Acura design team had to beat BMW. And they seem to have
done an excellent job. Chaparral Steel of Texas is a
leader in mini-mill technology. Its costs are among the
lowest in the U.S. steel industry, and lower even than
most of its overseas competitors. Chaparral can produce steel at about half what it costs a typical Japanese
mill. Founder Gordon Forward is technically trained
and experienced, but he doesn't have a research department. He reported in the Harvard Business Review:

> Our largest challenge is to cut the time it takes to get
> technology out of the lab and into operations. Let's go
> back to what I think happened at some of the bigger
> companies in the industry. Well, nothing happened.
> Sure, there was research. But I often thought that those
> companies had research departments just so CEOs
> could say something nice about technology in their an-
> nual reports. The companies all put in vice-presidents
> of research. The companies all built important-looking
> research centers, places with two thousand people in a
> spanking new facility out in Connecticut or somewhere,
> with fountains and lawns and little parks. Those places
> were lovely, really nice. But the first time I went into one

of them I though I was entering Forest Lawn. After you spend some time there, you realize you are in Forest Lawn. Not because there are no good ideas there, but because the good ideas are dying there all the time. Many of the ideas weren't all that hot. You know, someone would come up with a harebrained scheme that would burn out the refractory lining of a furnace. Now if this fellow had only had some production experience, he would know perfectly well that iron oxide, pure iron oxide, is a solvent for refractories. But chances are, he doesn't even talk to anybody in production.

I am not arguing that pure research has no place in our industry. But what we had was a lot of technical work that never got linked to real production needs. It was partly the fault of all those folks in the research centers, but it was also the fault of production people who were suspicious of any new ideas. They saw change as a challenge to their positions. They also treated the research people as safety valves. You can guess the way they thought: "If all those smart Ph.Ds are responsible for new ideas, we don't have to worry about them. Besides, most of the ideas are nonsense anyway. Just get out of our way and let us make the stuff we're supposed to make." It's what happens when you treat research as a staff operation.

So we've tried to bring research right into the factory and make it a line function. We make the people who are producing the steel responsible for keeping their process on the leading edge of technology worldwide. If they have to travel, they travel. If they have to figure out what the next step is, they go out and find the places where people are doing interesting things. They visit other companies (and other customers).

Regis McKenna, a renowned consultant to Silicon Valley companies, believes that every marketing person should be on the road a lot of the time to get that sixth sense that comes only from the marketplace. McKenna believes that, in this era of electronic communications, personal interaction is becoming more important than ever. He's right.

A Hewlett Packard engineer in integrated circuits said he spent almost all of his time working on applications on out-of-town-user premises rather than in his own laboratory.

Richard Schonberger in his book *World Class Manufacturing* writes: "Perhaps the biggest change of all for manufacturing engineering is getting used to the idea that the best way to make a contribution is found on the factory floor, not in the equipment manufacturers' catalogs. The manufacturing engineer must spend time with equipment sales representatives, but should spend more with machine operators, set-up crews, maintenance technicians and supervisors."

At Ben and Jerry's Ice Cream in Burlington, Vermont, the owners based their entire enterprise on the simple idea of giving the lovers of good ice cream more and more of what they want. Each new flavor, each innovative blend of textures, has to pass the test of ice-cream lovers and not just Ben and Jerry.

Allied-Signal's Lee Rivers knows that the level of basic research in this country is far more advanced and productive than anywhere else. Unfortunately, scientific leadership doesn't always produce the gain intended. In the ceramic industry, for example, U.S.

firms have worked to reduce the grain size of ceramic powders. And they have succeeded. But the Japanese have worked at the other end, at the point of application. The Japanese work directly with the user to develop useful new products. They know what is important to the end user. They are not as concerned about the more esoteric considerations of grain size in ceramics. They want to know what is needed to stand up under long periods of pounding and high heat. They go directly to improved product design and do this more efficiently then the highly skilled U.S. product developers, who are spending too much time in the laboratory and not enough time working in the front lines.

When the mind of the product developer is open to the front line and responds to it, the result will be far more new product successes than failures.

27. *New product successes come directly from an intense involvement with the market and an intense knowledge of competitive products.*

CHAPTER 18

Market Research Can't Replace Management Work in the Marketplace

MARKET RESEARCH is getting "smaller." Just a little bit of market research is often more than enough to guide the planning, to prod the decision making. Too much can bog down the entire process. Ideally, market research should be used to confirm what the management of the company already knows and believes. Market research should rarely be used to discover heretofore unknowns. When that occurs the company and its leaders have been locked in the home office far too long.

John Sculley now heads Apple Computer, and before that, he was a top executive at PepsiCo. His experience in these two very competitive industries has sharpened his dislike for too much research. He believes that the best marketing decisions are rarely made on the basis of quantitative research. Sculley says, "No great marketing decisions have ever been made on quantitative data."

We need to go no further than Coca-Cola, once Sculley's competitor, for a dramatic confirmation of his opinion about the limitations of quantitative market research. Coca-Cola determined through market research that the "softer, sweeter taste of Pepsi" had strong appeal, especially with the high-consuming youth market. Coke's characteristic "bite" appeared to be a problem with this part of the market. A product development plan was put in place. New Coke was launched nationwide and the result is now a "classic" in the lore of too much dependence on too much market research.

The other side of this story, however, can be found in the brilliant reversal decision by Coca-Cola management. Further research was not needed in their view. They knew that a mistake had been made and in a spectacular three-month turnaround, Classic Coke, that is, old Coke, was brought back. And in the process Coca-Cola's total share of market with New Coke and Classic Coke combined to take points away from Pepsi-Cola. (Of course it wasn't planned this way.)

Out of the bottomless swamp of market research has emerged a new creature, the focus group. The samples are smaller (very appealing) and the promise is greater. The rise of focus group research has blossomed. The best of it is done carefully with consumers selected to be "representative" of the total market. They are brought together for a discussion of the product or the service. The key to focus-group research rests in the ability of the moderator to manage the discussion, to sort through the various opinions and finally to draw some significant conclusion for the marketing of the product or service. The idea seems bright enough, the sample is small, the costs are reasonable. But the results are opinionated, because a major problem is that one "talker," one strong personality, can lead and influence the focus group.

This kind of market research has, unfortunately, come to be the equivalent of social lunch conversations for groups of ten to twelve.

Where did the love affair with quantitative research develop? In part, it came directly from the growth of home-office staffs. It came directly from the expanded staff departments in all types of research from product to consumer to media to advertising. The sophistication and refinement in the various disciplines of research have grown year after year. The research department can become a world apart, a world that rests on facts in volume. And it becomes difficult to argue against this type of material. "The facts are there for all to see," as one manager reported to me.

It is significant that the growth of quantitative research has also coincided with the growth of the business schools. Graduates poured into home-office staffs all during the 1950s, 1960s and 1970s, and they still do. But the reverence for the methodology learned by the MBAs has begun to recede somewhat lately.

Someone has suggested throwing bricks through the windows of MBA staffers, bricks wrapped in re-

28. *Market research has advanced to the point of richly elaborated confusion.*

search reports from samples of ten thousand or more. I have been through the quantitative research phase and opted instead for highly personal interactive research with consumers by product development people, by marketing people and, most important, by top management. Customer information from a small sample received by the right minds can do wonders in guiding a business. The number in the sample is not what is important. It is the quality of this interactive research that counts. It is just one more example of what can happen when there is one-to-one work on the front line by people who have the responsibility not only to get the exposure, but to come to the right conclusions as a result.

One company I have worked with has started to use its telephone service center as a source for information on the market, on its products and on the products of competitors. Once the requested service is handled, the operators use the opportunity to ask five questions about the market, the products and the competition and finally to seek suggestions from the callers on what the company can do to do a better job. Here is direct-response market research that costs very little and, in total, gives to management a significant amount of useful market information.

Staff people had developed wrong attitudes toward the various people in the chain of distribution, in shipping, in selling, in wholesaling and in retailing. These attitudes were expressed with comments like, "What can I possibly learn from those guys?" The answer, of course, is plenty—if you are smart enough to ask the right questions and to listen very hard to the responses.

In *The Initiative Manager*, Roy Ravan reports a conversation with a manager of a data service company: "I've never been surprised by research. Research is more of a confirmation tool than a discovery tool."

In some businesses, the leaders have recognized the need to get closer to the market to find out what is happening and what is needed. So the idea of retail advisory committees was developed. Committees have been formed with car dealers, supermarkets, drug chains, appliance stores and so on. There are hundreds of these advisory committee meetings held across the country every year. The intent is for the sponsoring company to use the committee to get closer to the market. Unfortunately, this approach has the same value, the same built-in problem, as does focus-group research with consumers, only worse. The meeting does not become an opportunity for the frankest type of discussion about what is right and what is wrong. Theoretically, retailer advisory committees are used to learn from the front line. But the truth is that the intent has less to do with a deep desire to learn from the market than a desire to show the customers "we do listen to you and we do try to give you more of what you want to help you sell more." No one knows this better than members of the advisory committees. They know why they are there and they know all too well what they should say and what they should not say. In contrast, one-to-one contact with people in the front line can provide the research that management needs.

CHAPTER 19

Upping the Incentives

THE TROUBLE with comprehensive benefit plans is that, like clean rest rooms, they soon become accepted as the norm and no longer serve as the incentives they were designed to be. Though the list varies from company to company, most plans include medical benefits, pension plans, profit-sharing plans, extended vacation time, 401K plans and stock option plans. The longer the employee stays, the greater the buildup of benefits.

The other side of the picture is cash as the direct reward for performance. Do a great job and get a chunk of cash. Now. Today. And thanks. And let's do it again.

Many executive incentive plans don't go deep enough into the organization. Nor do they necessarily reward real performance. Here was an especially grotesque example: During a year when a downturn in earnings at General Motors eliminated profit-sharing payments to production workers, executives, in a different plan, earned huge bonuses. Ross Perot, who was then affiliated with GM, said in *Time* magazine in 1988, "You can't look the troops in the eye and say, 'It's been a bad year; we can't do anything for you,' but then say, 'By the way, we're going to pay ourselves a $1 million bonus.'"

A growing number of companies are working to push the dollar incentive down into the ranks, into the plants, the branch offices, the sales organization. No one formula or approach will work for every company or category of employee. But whatever system is chosen, it should be about cash for performance. Here are some of the characteristics such programs should include. They represent the thinking of Robert Townsend, in his book *Further Up the Organization*, and other smart observers regarding what causes people to perform better:

1. Any plan you propose to install must be in writing and in all respects clearly defined. It must have clear and manageable operating statements (using generally accepted accounting principles) so that the manager and his key people (the more the better) can know month by month how they are doing. And, of course, it should be fair and have reasonable expectations of payout. It is foolish to install a plan with goals and rewards that can't reasonably be achieved. And there should be no ceilings on the rewards. Every employee in the plan should understand what is being proposed and what can be gained for effective work.

Wherever possible, the profit center should be the focus. The earnings of a manager of a profit center should bear a direct relationship to the center's performance.

2. Top management incomes should express clearly the attitude of the company in rewarding performance. The top people should have base salaries in the same range. Keeping the difference among the CEO and his four or five key people to ten thousand dollars or less can have a powerful effect toward fostering teamwork and reducing friction at the top. Paying the CEO double or triple the bonus of the chief operating officer or the chief financial officer says that the company doesn't understand incentives.

3. One approach is to establish for the long term a precise percent of pretax profit, 10, 13 percent, whatever makes sense, to be divided among the profit-center group.

4. Avoid discretionary bonuses; they just demonstrate that a company doesn't understand how rational incentives work.

5. The incentive plan should have a formula that remains the same or nearly so from year to year. Employees in the plan must all be identified at the start of each operating year. Those not covered because their work isn't good enough should be out of the company altogether.

6. The key to your incentive plan is the rating system, which should, in general, reflect base salary levels. Participants should have specific ratings

that indicate the share of the incentive that each is to receive. No employee should be excluded, though bottom-level people will be assigned low share ratings. But, if at all practical, they should be included, even if the rewards are small. It's not only the reward for a particular year but the potential for a higher rating that will drive every employee.

7. Make the plan permanent, and once you have created and refined your plan, leave it alone. Don't adjust it because the payments become "too high." The higher the reward, the better the business is doing. Don't try to "correct" the plan at this point. Let those who earn big rewards enjoy them and try for even bigger ones. That's what it's all about.

8. Don't try to adjust the plan for "factors beyond our control" when something you couldn't foresee sends your business soaring or plummeting. Oil embargos, famines, booms and busts will always intrude on your planning. Pay what the plan says, whatever it says, whether it is more or less than people deserved.

9. Changes in the plan should be held to a minimum. If you have to give a special reward for performance so outstanding and distinctive that the plan doesn't provide for it, consider putting it in the form of a raise in base pay instead of making some ad hoc alteration of the plan.

Every profit-center program can reflect the needs of the operation and the people. The variations in such a plan are endless. The members of groups can be expanded. Perhaps the key decision is in the percent of the incentive shared by each group. It is possible to push the incentive down into the lower grades by adjusting the incentive share for each group. There is an inherent message in such a program that can increase productivity throughout the entire organization. The practice of "creaming" by top management (in the short term) is obliterated. This message is almost as powerful as the money involved.

The partners benefit at about equal levels. Team work is fostered. The desire to help each other becomes important.

Above all, keep the plan simple. Don't bring in compensation consultants. Develop the plan directly from an intimate knowledge of the organization and the people involved. Measure the simplicity of the plan by making it clearly understandable to the lowest group in the plan. If they get it and work for it, the plan is a good one.

29. *What such an incentive program does is create a partnership approach at the top of the organization.*

CHAPTER 20

There's a Way to Make Better Use of the Brightest and the Best

EDWARD WRAPP, business policy professor at the University of Chicago, suggests that we have created a monster. The business schools have done more to insure the success of the Japanese and West German invasion of America than any other thing. Wrapp deplores the business schools' overemphasis on quantitative methods, and I am in full agreement with him.

The enormous growth of home-office staffs beginning in the 1950s took place at the same time as the growth of business school graduates, the now-ubiquitous MBAs. And that of course was no accident. Each year home-office staffs grew as the business schools poured out their graduates.

Most of those who did not choose Wall Street ended up on corporate home-office staffs. John Gould, dean of the University of Chicago's graduate business school, reports that 25 percent of recent graduates chose investment banking for their first jobs. MBAs certainly are trained to analyze and evaluate financial plans.

Leaving Wall Street–bound MBAs aside, it is reasonable to ask how well those who enter other kinds of business are trained for what they must deal with and how well they are used in contemporary business.

Dana's René McPherson turned a company in a traditional unionized industry into a front-runner in productivity and then became dean of the Stanford University graduate school of business. One of his colleagues, who was an associate dean, said, "I've just had my first long meeting with René. He talked to me about his Dana experience. Do you know that not one thing he did there is even mentioned in the MBA curriculum?"

Gary Grattlieb, professor at NYU's business school, believes that students today want formulas and methodology and this comes in a two-year package. It is interesting to note that Dr. Grattlieb left his tenured teaching job at NYU to do research on mortgage-backed securities for an investment banker.

Journalist Steve Lohr concluded in a New York *Times* article "that there is a widely held view that the MBA might be part of the current problem in American industry."

Michael Thomas, novelist, art historian and former investment banker, has said in a New York *Times* article, "They lack liberal arts literacy . . . need a broader vision, a sense of history, perspectives from literature and art. I'd close every one of the graduate schools of business."

A *Business Week* writer put the case succinctly: "Most MBA-style top management lacks a gut feeling for the gestalt of their business."

A National Semiconductor manager reports, "People with degrees like a Harvard MBA and a Stanford MBA last about seventeen months. They can't cope with the flexibility and lack of structure."

Another senior management man in the computer industry comes down hard against business-school training with this quote: "They teach that well-trained managers can manage anything. They promoted a detached, analytical justification for decisions. This is right enough to be dangerous. It has led us seriously astray."

Here's another comment from Professor Wrapp: "The system is producing a horde of managers with demonstrable talents, but talents that are not in the mainstream of the enterprise. Professional managers are willing to study, analyze and define the problem. They are steeped in specialization, standardization, efficiency, productivity and quantification. They are highly rational and analytical. They insist on objective goals. In some organizations, they can succeed if they are simply good at making presentations to the board of directors or writing strategies or plans.

"The tragedy is that these talents mask real deficiencies in overall management capabilities. These talented performers run for cover when grubby operating decisions must be made and often fail miserably when they are charged with earning a profit, getting things done and moving an organization forward."

Here's another knowing comment from a CEO: "The word strategy used to mean a good idea for knocking off the competition. More recently it has often come to be synonymous with the quantitative breakthrough, the analytic coup, market share numbers, learning curve theory."

But there are signs of hope. Courses in strategy are starting to recognize and address the problem of implementation. Courses in manufacturing are coming back into fashion. Finance departments are still as strong as ever in the business schools. But teachers and students in sales management and manufacturing—the core disciplines of most businesses—are still scarce.

A great many of these MBAs started on their track to move up to executive vice-president or president or chairman. It was logical. Business-school training had prepared them to think of the management of a business from the top. The case-history method evaluated company performance from the point of view of what management did or did not do, the overall plan for the business, the strategies that were used to guide the business, where the business succeeded and where it failed.

Businesses successfully oriented to the front line can make the most of the talent coming out of the business schools by providing an environment that will benefit them for all their working years. Here are some ways to make the most of new MBAs:

1. Make it clear from the first interview that the new MBA won't get a home office staff job.
2. Regardless of their chosen discipline in business school, put new MBAs into production or field sales jobs, even if they want eventually to work in finance. The experience gained in the market-place or on the shop floor will provide indispensable insights into what capital really finances.
3. Help the MBA to understand how the company works and to gain respect for the people down the line who make things and money.
4. Help the MBA to recognize the qualities of the people in the company who created the business and made it grow even under conditions of high pressure, qualities that he or she is not likely to have encountered at business school.

CHAPTER *21*

Use of Consultants Is a Sure Sign That Management Is Weak

THE CONSULTANT lives and works with sand castles, temporary structures that are washed away after the report, the "big book," is delivered to the client company's top management. Consultants lead vicarious lives. They play CEO-for-a-day. And then they are gone, leaving the people in the company to take the "big book" with its recommendations and try to achieve the results promised.

Companies oriented to the front line rarely need consultants. Their top executives are close enough to the marketplace, the distribution, the pricing, the gross profit margins, the new product development so they are rarely surprised by the results they achieve in sales and profit. They know the results even before they get the reports. They work where the results are achieved, so they can see them as they happen. They know the plans, the actions, the new products. They know what worked and what did not work. And most important, they know why. I am convinced that top executives of companies who have to use consultants are too lazy or dumb to do the job themselves.

Yet consultants prosper. In fact in California, a new consulting firm was recently formed to consult with consulting companies to help them do a better consulting job.

The world of consultants is a paper world. Everything comes down to the "big book," the report to the client. The charts, diagrams, the facts and figures (and now the color slides and videos) are all part of the consultant's product. The people in this world of consultants are talented, well trained and well paid. But they are at least once removed from the real issues of the business they are consulting with. That is often merchandised by consultants as an advantage; by being somewhat removed from the arena, they bring a "fresh" look. But that simply is merchandising their ignorance.

I would rather save the big fees. The problem is not with the consultants and the work they do. The problem is with a company whose management believes that consultants are needed, because those executives do not work closely enough to the front line to know their business. They need help. They need information. They need ideas. They need problems defined. They need solutions. They need all of these things because they are not doing their jobs. So they bring in consultants to help develop strategies for growth.

Of course, in such specialized areas as factory design, production methods and new financing sources, consultants such as engineers and investment bankers can be useful. But the broader the consultant's assignment, the more it becomes an indictment of the management.

One of the stranger aspects of the consulting process is that much of the information these people use comes from inside the company. Where else can it come from for projects in production and marketing strategy, product design, organization structure, personnel development and so on?

Companies need constantly to reassess where they are and where they are going. But for those oriented to the front line, that is an ongoing process. And when a study is required, an outside consultant need not be called in. Instead create a project team within the company. This team can do the fact gathering and make recommendations to management. Assign as the leader of the project an executive with enough power and integrity to override the office politics.

This project group must not only make recommendations but also must be responsible for putting them to work. That is where this procedure differs from that of the traditional consultant relationship. It is why smart companies produce their own studies and reports on special projects, when they really need them. They don't have to use the kinds of compelling communication devices that consultants use to titillate the client company's management.

For example, one consultant, McKinsey & Co., uses

something called the 7–S diagram to define the seven factors that it considers to be the criteria for success in a business. By stretching a little, the consulting firm manages to get all of these seven factors to begin with an "S." One professor at the Harvard business school urged the company to present it that way, indicating that without the "memory blocks" provided by the alliteration of the Ss, the whole idea was too hard to explain "and easily forgettable" (his words). They are not only forgettable; they are typical of the tricks and nonsense that consultants use to sell their services. The seven variables are structure, system, style, staff, skills, strategy and shared values. Cute, isn't it? And you get to pay big bucks to be treated like a child.

The consultants look inside the company and spread far and wide in search of the information they need. But what they see and hear is different from what top management will get by following exactly the same paths. If the project is a large and vital one to the company, then the use of a consultant firm can actually be harmful, because the consultant is learning what management should already know.

Look at the situation in realistic terms. If an experienced top manager is out in the marketplace listening and learning, how can the same route taken by a consultant come anywhere close to equaling what the company executive will learn? If the company executive is measuring what he learns in terms that directly affect the gross margins, for example, how can the consultant have a comparable mindset? After all, before the consultant has completed his report, a manager out on the front line will have used the information by taking the necessary action.

Unfortunately, corporate directors love the big, fact-loaded reports that consultants sell. They are often reassured by these neatly bound studies. In theory, they bring the business closer to the board. But a board that is guided by consultant reports is dangerous. Suddenly the members have more information about the operations of the business than they have ever had before. Board members come to meetings, hear the reports, read material provided, but rarely do they have the firsthand knowledge of the business they should have to make significant contributions. A consultant's report can convince board members that they know enough to begin to get more involved in operating decisions. And that can mean trouble for management and for the company.

CHAPTER *22*

Conclusion

THE MARKET-DRIVEN approach to leading and building a business puts some added burden on management. As I have tried to demonstrate in these pages, I am not talking simply about terms that have become the latest buzzwords of business lingo aimed at concealing realities. Being market-driven, in the sense that I am trying to convey, requires more energy and more effort. It involves more travel and more contact with more people. It requires the firm belief that the added effort is worth it. It requires a high regard for all the people in the marketplace. They all have to work effectively. They will do this when they know that management recognizes their work and respects them for doing it well. This is achieved by understanding the act of being there and talking to them and listening to what they have to say. They are not "the people down there."

They can and do make a difference by what they do and the way that they do it for the company.

For management this requires a level of openness and appreciation of the work being done. If the feeling is not real and deep rooted, people in the market will sense this. No amount of flashy glad-handing and posturing can cover up a lack of regard.

The final measure of how well the market-driven business works rests directly with the customers at all levels of the business. Do they like what they see and hear from the management people? Are they convinced that the meeting and talking and listening has a genuine purpose? Is there the sense that management is meeting with them with the goal of learning more about what the customer needs and wants? Does the customer sense that the purpose is to do an even better job for the customer? Running a market-driven business demands a respect for all of the people in the marketplace. If the conviction isn't there, save the time and the effort. Being market-driven only works when there is appreciation for all of the people who contribute to the success of the business in the marketplace.

But doing it and feeling and seeing it work can be the most satisfying, the most fulfilling experience anyone in business can ever enjoy.

Acknowledgments

There are many people who, over the years, have contributed to this book by their management style, by specific examples, by advice and by direct assistance. Those who have provided examples that are in this book include: Charles Ames, Acme Cleveland; J. Carter Bacot, Bank of New York; Leonwood Bean, L.L. Bean; Warren Ben-nis, University of Cincinnati; A. Bressler, Domino's Pizza; James Burke, Johnson & Johnson; Fletcher Byron, Koppers Corp.; Wes Canrell, Lanier; Ed Carlson, United Airlines; Bennett Cerf, Random House Publishing; Phillip Cooper, David Edward Limited; John Doyle, Hewlett Packard; Peter Drucker, Author & Teacher; Gordon Forward, Chaparral Steel; Ernest Gallo, Gallo Wines; Mikhail Gorbachev, Soviet Union; Peter Grace, Grace Corp.; Harry Gray, United Technologies; Robert Hall, Author; Michael Haverty, Atchison, Topeka RR; Kenneth Iverson, Nucor Corp.; Robert W. Johnson, Johnson & Johnson Corp.; Reginald Jones, General Electric; C.F. Kettering, General Motors; Charles Knight, Emerson Electric; Abe Krasnoff, Pall Corp.; Ray Kroc, McDonald's;

Allen Krow, IBM; Herman Lay, Frito-Lay; Dennis Marine, Harris Corp.; Willard Marriott, Sr., Marriott Corp.; Willard Marriott, Jr., Marriott Corp.; Ken Mason, Quaker Oats Co.; Regis McKenna, computer marketing consultant; René McPherson, Dana Corp.; Allen Mebone, Unifi Corp.; Joseph Metcalf, U.S. Navy; Roger Milliken, Milliken Textiles; Gene Milner,Lanier; Gerry Mitchell, Dana Corp.; Kenichi Ohmae, management consultant; Kenneth Olsen, Digital Equipment Corp.; David Packard, Hewlett Packard; Amos Parrish, Amos Parrish Company; John Patterson, NCR; Roger Penske, Penske Enterprises; Ross Perot, Perot Company; Tom Peters, author and lecturer; Donald Peterson, Ford Company; Roy Ravan, Author; Rose Marie Reed, Rose Marie Swim Suits; James Reid, Standard Products; Lee Rivers, Allied Signal; Francis (Buck) Rogers, IBM; Ted Santo, Dayton Power & Light; Julian Scheer, LTV; Michael Schulhof, Sony Corp of America; John Sculley, Apple Computer; Alfred Sloan, General Motors; Larry Small, Citicorp; Levi Strauss, Levi Strauss Corp.; Robert Townsend, Author & Lecturer; Fred Turner, McDonald's; Bill Turper, Texas Instruments; David Vogel, University of California; Sam Walton, Walmart; An Wang, Wang Laboratories; Stuart Watson, Heublein; Tom Wilson, Boeing; William Woodside, Primerica Corp.; Ed Wrapp, University of Chicago.

Also contributing are those executives I know who exemplify the basic premises of this book. They know the marketplace and how to work it and how to read it. I've worked with them as associates, as customers, as competitors. I have listed most of them by name only so that they know that I know and appreciate what they stand for. (I've probably missed some who should be included and they have my apologies.)

Don Aberg, Fred Adamany, Steve Albert, Drew Allen, Mark Armstrong, Michael Armstrong, Frank Ashcroft, Frank Avant, Dale Barley, Steve Barnhart, Dick Bazin, Bob Beatty, Pete Benzino, Don Bischoff, George Bishop, John Bland, Emery Bodnar, Gary Bolden, Jack Bolls, Bill Bridgeforth, Daryl Briggs, Tony Brocato, Bob Brockway, Bart Brodkin, Bill Brown, Carl Brown, Mike Brown, Roger Brown, Tom Brown, Steve Browne, John Budzak, Bill Bundy, Mike Buonasissi, Val Burlini, Nick Calico, Don Cameron, Dale Campbell, Bill Carron, Reuben Carter, Gus Christensen, Leon Clay, Ross Colbert, Royal Cole, Bob Coleman, Barksdale Collins, Mike Connellee, Bruce Conner, Rick Conway, Luke Cranford, Robert Curtis, Jr., Benny Dahlgreen, Wesley Davis Jr., Gary Davis, Jurrell Davis, Wes Davis, Dick Debosek, Lou Del Ponte, Buford Denton, Frank DiChiaro, Mike Dittrich, Tom Dooley, Chris Dunn, John DuPuis, Brian Dyson, Michael Eckes, Thomas Eddleman, Wes Elmer, John Evanson, Woody Faircloth, Tim Fallon, Gene Ferguson, Norm Findley, Jeff Fitzgerald, Ted Floca, Jim Flood, Jim Floyd, Dick Floyd, Mike Flynn, Pat Forgione, John Frazel, John Frazier, Tim French, Dan Furlow, Charlie Gagliano, Joe Garbarine, Butch Gibson, Marvin Goldstein, Tom Govert, Dick Graeber, Gary Green, John Gregory, Roy Gurvey, Les Haney, Dick Hazel, Dick Hegi, Bill Hemingway, Ike Herbert, Tom Hiles, Bill Hill, Frank Hill, Jim Hill,

Wayne Holcombe, Darrell Holland, Jack Holloway, Gene Honerman, Harold Honickman, Jeff Honickman, Don Hoyt, Al Hudgins, John Jiga, Skip Johnston, Bob Johnston, Oakley Jones, Mike Kaelin, George Kalil, Darold Keith, Jim Keown, Gus Kessler, Charlie King, A.L. Kirkpatrick, Jenny Kolls, Sandy Korschum, Bob Kriefels, Chris Kwong Yew, Bill Leader, Jim Lee, John Leen, Ed Leinweaver, Jim Lindsey, Joe Lombardo, Bob Lovell, Lou Lowenkron, John Lupo, Paul Manfredi, Jim Martin, Bill McCarey, Cole McCombs, Ray McCown, Jerry McGuire, Joel McNeil, Tony Mendes, Debbie Meredith, Michael Michaud, Norm Miller, Hoyt Minges, Tom Minges, John Minges, John Misser, Brent Mizell, Charles Moak, Harry Moser, Bruce Muenter, Fran Mullen, Buren Mullis, John Mynatt, Mike Naylor, Maynard Nehring, Gary Noack, Jim Nolan, Bob Nunnenkamp, John Osborne, Mike Parkes, J. Alfred Pate III, Frank Peck, Robert Poduch, Russ Ravens, Rick Ravens, Cliff Ritchie, Mark Ritchie, Lamar Rocker, Bob Ross, Bob Rough, Steve Roughton, Danny Rye, Mauricio Saca, Emilio Saca, Larry Sanford, Roger Schilling, Henry Schimberg, Gary Schirripa, Mark Schortman, Mike Schramm, Steve Schreiber, Steve Schriner, Ron Sellers, Steve Sheckengaust, Henry Sherry, Harry Shippey, Larry Shoemaker, John Shurman, Homer Sledge, Gary Sligar, Dennis Smith, Mark Smith, Larry Smith, Richard Sok, Rick Spingler, Larry Stanford, Doug Stark, Jim Stevens, Peter Steward, Tom Stewart, Jerry Streva, Lisa Streva, Joe Stutz, Charlie Sullivan, Toby Summers, Stan Sweitzer, John Taglienti, John Taylor, Rick

Thomas, Charlie Thomas, John Thorp, Ken Timms, Eldred Tippins, Michael E. Tomlinson, Jim Turner, Jake Vallarino III, Don Veechi, Jorge Vilor, Jim Waldron, Neal Wallace, Ken Walz, Russ Watters, Jim Welch, Bob Westerfield, Dude Whitfield, Ray Williams, Sandy Williams, Don Wilson, Don Wissink, Randy Wissink, Ken Witzman, Jim Woods, Charles Young, Dave Zittsman

I especially appreciate the insightful editing and the critical comments and ideas that Stanley H. Brown has provided. The objective from the start was to produce a book that will have an impact on management in the future.